GO GET A WOOLLY HAT

An Account of the Recovery of Kursk Submarine

Adrian Ladd

authorHOUSE®

AuthorHouse™ UK Ltd.
500 Avebury Boulevard
Central Milton Keynes, MK9 2BE
www.authorhouse.co.uk
Phone: 08001974150

First published by AuthorHouse 8/18/2009

ISBN: 978-1-4490-1642-5 (sc)

This book is printed on acid-free paper.

THIS BOOK IS DEDICATED TO ALL THE SAILORS WHO LOST THEIR LIFE IN THOSE 9 COMPARTMENTS OF THE KURSK AND THE CREW OF THE DSND MAYO AND ONSHORE SUPPORT WHO ENDEAVOURED TO RECOVER HER

1st Compartment

1. Senior Midshipman Abdulkadyr M. Il'darov - leading torpedoman (Dagestan Rep.)
2. Midshipman Aleksey V. Zubov - hydroacoustic party technician (Ukraine)
3. Seaman Ivan N. Nefedkov - torpedo section commander (Sverdlovsk Reg.)
4. Seaman Maksim N. Borzhov - torpedoman (Vladimir Reg.)
5. Seaman Aleksey V. Shul'gin - bilge artificer (Arkhangelsk Reg.)
6. Senior Lieutenant Arnold Yu. Borisov - attached from OAO "Dagdizel" Plant (Dagestan Rep.)
7. Mamed I. Gadzhiyev - attached from OAO "Dagdizel" Plant (Dagestan Rep.)

2nd Compartment

Staff of the 7th Submarine Division

1. Captain 1 rank Vladimir T. Bagriantsev - chief of 7-th Submarine Division Staff (Crimea Rep.)
2. Captain 2 rank Yuriy T. Shepetnov - missile flag officer (Crimea Rep.)
3. Captain 2 rank Viktor M. Belogun' - deputy chief of Division Engineering Service (Ukraine)
4. Captain 2 rank Vasiliy S. Isayenko - assistant chief of Division Engineering Service (Crimea Rep.)
5. Captain 3 rank Marat I. Baygarin - acting torpedo flag officer (Saint Petersburg)

Crew

6. Captain 1 rank Gennadiy P. Liachin - commanding officer (Volgograd Reg.)
7. Captain 2 rank Sergey V. Dudko - first officer (Byelorussia)
8. Captain 2 rank Aleksandr A. Shubin - upbringing officer (Crimea Rep.)
9. Captain-Lieutenant Maksim A. Safonov - navigating officer (Moscow Reg.)
10. Senior Lieutenant Sergey N. Tylik - electric navigation party commander (Murmansk Reg.)
11. Senior Lieutenant Vadim Ya Bubniv - electric navigation party engineer (Ulyanovsk Reg.)
12. Captain 3 rank Andrey B. Silogava - missile officer (Crimea Rep.)
13. Captain-Lieutenant Aleksey V. Shevchuk - commander of control party, missile dept. (Murmansk Reg.)
14. Senior Lieutenant Andrey V. Panarin - engineer of control party of missile dept. (Leningrad Reg.)
15. Senior Lieutenant Boris V. Geletin - commander of launch party of missile dept. (Murmansk Reg.)
16. Senior Leiutenant Sergey V. Uzkiy - commander, target designation party, missile dept. (Arkhangelsk)
17. Captain 2 rank Yuriy B. Sablin - engineering officer (Crimea Rep.)
18. Captain 3 rank Andrey V. Miliutin - damage-control assistant (Saint Petersburg)
19. Captain-Lieutenant Sergey S. Kokurin - commander, bilge party damage-control division (Voronezh Reg.)

20. Midshipman Vladimir V. Khivuk - mustering technician (Kursk Reg.)
21. Captain 3 rank Aleksandr Ye. Sadkov - control officer (Amur Reg.)
22. Captain-Lieutenant Mikhail O. Rodionov - computer party commander (Crimea Rep.)
23. Senior Lieutenant Sergey N. Yerahtin - computer party engineer (Murmansk Reg.)
24. Midshipman Yakov V. Samovarov - chief of sanitary section (Arkhangelsk Reg.)
25. Senior Midshipman Aleksandr V. Ruzliov - ship's boatswain (Murmansk Reg.)
26. Midshipman Konstantin V. Kozyrev - electric navigation party technician (Murmansk Reg.)
27. Senior Midshipman Vladimir V. Fesak - electric navigation party technician, missile department (Ukraine)
28. Midshipman Andrey N. Polianskiy - electric navigation party technician, torpedo dept. (Krasnodar Reg.)
29. Midshipman Segrey A. Kislinskiy - technician of launch party of missile department (Kostroma Reg.)
30. Midshipman Sergey V. Griaznyh - computer party technician (Arkhangelsk Reg.)
31. Seaman Dmitriy S. Mirtov - steersman-signaller (Komi Rep.)
32. Petty Officer 2 class (under contract) Dmitriy A. Leonov - steersman,signallers sect. commander
(Moscow)
33. Senior Lieutenant Maksim A. Rvanin - engineering party engineer (Arkhangelsk Reg.)
34. Seaman Andrey N. Driuchenko - electrician (Arkhangelsk Reg.)
35. Senior Lieutenant Aleksey A. Ivanov-Pavlov - torpedo officer (Ukraine)
36. Midshipman Viktor A. Paramonenko - hydroacoustic party technician (Ukraine)

3rdCompartment

1. Captain-Lieutenant Dmitriy A. Repnikov - assistant commanding officer (Crimea Rep.)
2. Captain 3 rank Andrey A. Rudakov - Commander of Military Unit 4 , signal officer (Moscow Reg.)
3. Captain-Lieutenant Sergey G. Fiterer - space communication party commander (Kaliningrad Reg.)
4. Captain-Lieutenant Oleg I. Nosikovskiy - classified automatic communication party commander
   (Kaliningrad.)
5. Captain-Lieutenant Vitaliy M. Solorev - commander of equipment party of damage-control division (Bryansk)
6. Captain-Lieutenant Sergey N. Loginov - hydroacoustic party commander (Ukraine)
7. Captain-Lieutenant Andrey V. Koroviakov - hydroacoustic party engineer, navigator's dept. (St Petersburg)
8. Captain-Lieutenant Aleksey V. Korobkov - hydroacoustic party engineer, missile dept. (Murmansk Reg.)
9. Captain-Lieutenant Aleksandr V. Gudkov - radio intelligence party commander (Kaliningrad Reg.)
10. Captain 3 rank Viacheslav A. Bezsokirnyy - chief of chemical service (Ukraine)

11. Senior Midshipman Igor' V. Yerasov - crypto operator (Voronezh Reg.)
12. Senior Midshipman Vladimir V. Svechkariov - telegraphy operator, classified automatic communication
    (Nizhny Novgorod Reg.)
13. Senior Midshipman Sergey A. Kalinin - telegraphy operator, classified automatic communication, missile
    dept. (Ukraine)
14. Senior Midshipman Igor V. Fedorichev - control department technician (Tula Reg.)
15. Midshipman Maksim I. Vishniakov - target designation party technician (Ukraine)
16. Midshipman Segrey S. Chernyshov - space communication party technician (Crimea Rep.)
17. Midshipman Mikhail A. Belov - hydroacoustic party technician (Nizhny Novgorod Reg.)
18. Midshipman Pavel V. Tavolzhanskiy - hydroacoustic party technician (Belgorod Reg.)
19. Senior Midshipman Sergey B. Vlasov - radio intelligence party technician (Murmansk Reg.)
20. Midshipman Sergey A. Rychkov - chemical service technician (Uzbekistan)
21. Petty Officer 2 class (under contract) Yuriy A. Annenkov - Mechanic of Military Unit 2 (Kursk Reg.)
22. Seaman Dmitriy A. Kotkov - missile department mechanician (Vologda Reg.)
23. Dubbing Seaman Nikolay V. Pavlov - missile department mechanician (Voronezh Reg.)
24. Seaman Ruslan V. Trianichev - bilge artificer (Vologda Reg.)

4thCompartment

1. Senior Lieutenant Denis S. Kirichenko - damage-control engineer (Ulyanovsk Reg.)
2. Captain of Medical service Aleksey B. Stankevich - medical officer (Ukraine, Saint Petersburg)
3. Midshipman Vitaliy F. Romaniuk - surgeon's assistant (Crimea Rep.)
4. Senior Midshipman Vasiliy V. Kichkiruk - head of sanitary team (Ukraine)
5. Senior Midshipman Anatoliy N. Beliayev - ship's cook (instructor) (Ryazan Reg.)
6. Chief ship's Petty Officer /under contract/ Salovat V. Yasapov - cook (instructor) (Bashkortostan Rep.)
7. Seaman Sergey A. Vitchenko - cook (Leningrad Reg.)
8. Seaman Oleg V. Yevdokimov - cook (Kursk Reg.)
9. Seaman Dmitry V. Starosel'tsev - bilge seaman (Kursk Reg.)
10. Seaman Aleksandr V. Halepo - turbine stand-by operator (Komi Rep.)
11. Seaman Aleksey Yu. Kolomeytsev - turbine stand-by operator (Komi Rep.)
12. Seaman Igor' V. Loginov - turbine stand-by operator (Komi Rep.)

5thCompartment

1. Captain 3 rank Dmitriy B. Murachiov - party commander of main propulsion division (Crimea Rep.)
2. Captain-Lieutenant Denis S. Pshenichnikov - party commander, control division, navigator's

dept. (Crimea)

3. Captain-Lieutenant Sergey N. Liubushkin - party commander, control division, missile dept. (N. Novgorod)

4. Captain 3 rank Ilya V. Shchavinskiy - engineering division commander (Saint Petersburg)

5. Captain-Lieutenant Aleksandr Ye. Vasilyev - commander, equipment party, main propulsion division (Crimea)

6. Captain 3 rank Nikolay A. Beloziorov - engineering party commander (Voronezh Reg.)

7. Senior Midshipman Ivan I. Tsymbal - technician-electrician (Ukraine)

8. Midshipman Oleg V. Troyan - chemical service technician (Azerbaijan)

9. Chief Petty Officer (under contract) Aleksandr V. Neustroyev - electrician (Tomsk Reg.)

10. Seaman Aleksey A. Larionov - bilge seaman (Komi Rep.)

11. Midshipman Vladimir G. Shablatov - technician-electrician (Mari El Rep.)

5thBis Compartment

1. Senior Lieutenant Vitaliy Ye. Kuznetsov - engineering party engineer, navigator's dept. (Novgorod Reg.)

2. Senior Midshipman Nail' Kh. Khafizov - leading instructor of chemical service (Bashkortostan Rep.)

3. Senior Midshipman Yevgeniy Yu. Gorbunov - diesel operator (Nizhny Novgorod reg.)

4. Midshipman Valeriy A. Baybarin - head of bilge team of damage-control division (Chelyabinsk Reg.)

6thCompartment

1. Captain-Lieutenant Rashid R. Ariapov - main propulsion assistant (Uzbekistan)

2. Midshipman Aleksey G. Balanov - head of bilge team of main propulsion division (Chuvash Rep.)

3. Senior Lieutenant Aleksey V. Mitiayev - engineer, equipment party, main propulsion division (St.Petersburg)

4. Chief Petty Officer (under contract) Viacheslav V. Maykagashev - bilge specialist (Khakass Rep.)

5. Seaman Aleksey A. Korkin - bilge specialist (Arkhangelsk Reg.)

7thCompartment

1. Captain-Lieutenant Dmitriy R. Kolesnikov - commander, technical party, main propulsion division
    (St.Petersburg)

2. Midshipman Fanis M. Ishmuradov - technical party technician (Bashkortostan Rep.)

3. Petty Officer 2 class (under contract) Vladimir S. Sadovoy - turbine section commander (N. Novgorod Reg.)

4. Seaman Roman V. Kubikov - turbine operator (Kursk Reg.)
5. Seaman Aleksey N. Nekrasov - turbine operator (Kursk Reg.)
6. Petty Officer 1 class /under contract/ Reshid R. Zubaydullin - electrician (Ulyanovsk Reg.)
7. Seaman Ilya S. Naliotov - turbine operator (Vologda Reg.)
8. Petty Officer 2 class /under contract/ Roman V. Anikiyev - turbine operator (Murmansk Reg.)
9. Senior Midshipman Vladimir A. Kozadiorov - technician & turbine operator (Lipetsk Reg.)

8thCompartment

1. Captain-Lieutenant Sergey V. Sadilenko - party engineer of control division, navigator's department (Ukraine)
2. Senior Midshipman Viktor V. Kuznetsov - turbine operator mate (Kursk Reg.)
3. Chief ship's Petty Officer /under contract/ Robert A. Gesler - turbine section commander (Bashkortostan Rep.)
4. Senior Midshipman Andrey M. Borisov - technician, equipment party, main propulsion division (Ryazan)
5. Seaman Roman V. Martynov - turbine operator (Komi Rep.)
6. Seaman Viktor Yu. Sidiuhin - turbine operator (Komi Rep.)
7. Seaman Yuriy A. Borisov - turbine operator (Komi Rep.)

9thCompartment

1. Senior Lieutenant Aleksandr V. Brazhkin - party engineer of control division, missile department (Crimea Rep.)
2. Midshipman Vasiliy E. Ivanov - head of electricians' team (Mari El Rep.)
3. Midshipman Mikhail A. Bochkov - technician of bilge party of damage-control division (Crimea Rep.)

THE RUSSIAN NUCLEAR SUBMARINE FLEET

The second time the needle jerked it measured 3.5 on the Richter scale - equivalent to the detonation of about one and a half tons of high explosive . Personnel in seismic stations as far a field as northern Norway, Canada and Alaska picked up the signal (the first, some two minutes earlier, had measured 1.5 on the Scale - equivalent to the detonation of about 100 kgs. of high explosive) and recognised that this event, at 7.32 GMT on the12th August 2000, was a serious occurrence. Somewhere in the northern ocean there had been a mighty explosion. Two US submarines, USS Memphis and USS Toledo, and one British submarine, HMS Splendid, all in the area of the Barents Sea to shadow Russian military manoeuvres, simultaneously detected the blasts.

On that morning the Russian Northern Fleet Command, on exercise in the Barents Sea , lost contact with one of its mightiest nuclear- powered submarine cruisers - K141 "Kursk" - in international waters about 250 kms east of Kirkenes in north-east Norway some 135 kms off Severmorsk in Russia. This is not just the story of the demise of the "Kursk", how and why she sank, but how she was eventually raised from the seabed. It recounts the huge problems facing those who attempted to rescue the crew of the submarine and those who later successfully raised the vessel. It also highlights the courage of the salvage divers, and the comrade of the people, who were to undertake what one reporter described as "the most dangerous job on earth".

Before the "Kursk" sank, there were already five nuclear submarine abandoned on the ocean floors. Two were American - the "Thresher", lost in 1963, and the "Scorpion", lost in 1968. The other three were Russian. K-8 went down in 1970; K-219 in 1986; and K-278 "Komsomolets" sank in 1989. They were all far too deep to raise to the surface (at depths between 1685m and 5000m) and all were assumed to be safe from serious radioactive leakage for many years to come. (No one knows, however, what the long term effects of great underwater pressures will be on the reactor chambers of those submarines.) The "Kursk" was very different. When she was detected, sometime on the 13th August, she lay on the seabed at a depth of only 116metres and, unlike the other doomed submarines, in a major fishing area. The ecological consequences for the northern seas and for the food chain around the entire Arctic Circle were immeasurable. Moreover, though no one could be certain, there was every chance that some or all of the personnel on board were alive. True she had not sent out any radio distress messages nor had any emergency buoys been spotted in her vicinity but there were hopes of rescuing survivors. This hope was mixed with incredulity that the personnel on such a seemingly impregnable vessel could possibly be lost.

But perhaps that incredulity was misplaced. If people had understood the system under which the "Kursk", and her sister ships in the Russian nuclear fleet, had been built and commissioned they might have been able to comprehend more clearly the possible reasons for her terrible fate: the reasons, indeed, for why and how she sank.

The Russians have now lost twice as many nuclear submarines as the Americans, to say nothing of numerous serious accidents stopping just short of out and out loss of vessels. Admittedly the Russian nuclear submarine fleet is the largest in the world, but is there anything in the Russian system which would explain this poor record? Years before the "Kursk" disaster the Oslo- based Bellona Foundation published a chillingly analytical report on the Russian Northern Fleet: much of what follows in the next few pages is drawn from its findings. In this book, with very few exceptions, the word "Russian" is used to describe both Soviet and Russian periods. Although not strictly accurate to keep changing from one to the other would be confusing, but it must be understood that the period before refers to the "USSR" and the "Soviet" period.

The report took as its premise that there were three main factors contributing to the safe operation and use of nuclear submarines. Firstly, the quality of the design and construction of the vessels, their ammunition and technical equipment. Secondly, the skill in the operation of the submarine and the use of pertinent technology over the course of the vessels' lifetimes. And thirdly, the professional training of the crew and the professional administration of the work needed on those submarines. On each of these three counts the report (Report No.2: 1996 of the Bellona Foundation, "The Russian Northern Fleet," **The Nuclear Chronicle from Russia**, Oslo, 1996.) found the Russian record was seriously at fault. The antecedents of the system that created many of the problems for the Russians dated back many decades. In the old USSR a patchwork of ministries, committees and councils administered the building and delivery of military hardware and this system is only slowly being reformed. The navy, for instance, had no say in the quality control and safety requirements of its nuclear submarines. It had to accept whatever vessels were provided for it. .For their part, like all the providers of weaponry for the armed services, the builders of submarines faced enormous time constraints. They were allowed no flexibility: even if a vessel was incomplete or had not undergone sea trials it had to be delivered on time, in line with a rigid timetable. Sometimes submarines arrived on station without all the necessary safety equipment, or with specifications so altered that parts were missing or defective. In 1989, for example, there were 529 different complaints about nuclear submarines being delivered with faulty equipment. In 1990-91 the navy returned a new submarine to the building yard because of the numerous defects in its mechanical equipment. Another vessel was commissioned without light switches in the cabins or missile Compartments.

To compound such problems, different authorities ran the servicing and repair yards. This meant that there was a lack of standardisation of tools and equipment and often a shortage of spare parts. Hence the quality and safety of repairs and upgrading were compromised. From the planning stage to final delivery, the system was plagued by inefficiencies and muddle.

As a consequence of all these defects during the submarines' operational lives more accidents occurred than was acceptable in a modern fighting fleet. Poor maintenance, disregard for instructions, and improper procedures for using technical equipment and ammunition, all contributed to a sorry record. Crews often lacked the required levels of training, especially to ensure the survivability of a submarine. One commander, indeed, complained to his superiors that 11 of his 23 new crew members could not speak Russian and so were incapable of working with the nuclear reactors. As a consequence the crews often lacked the experience to foresee potential critical situations. One observer, indeed, later contended that it was inferior crew training that lead to the fate that befell the "Kursk".

Yet despite all these drawbacks in 1996, when the Bellona Foundation issued their report, Russia still lead the world in submerged speed and deep diving submarines. Obviously she had many experienced and highly dedicated submariners and designers, yet they were impeded by systems that often lead to frustration and mishap. Coupled to this were the working conditions of the seamen who often endured considerable physical and psychological overload. Their irregular working hours and rest periods added up to a combination which brought together all the ingredients to turn small accidents into major catastrophes.

Although the report appeared in 1996 the picture it painted had in some essentials deteriorated by the time the "Kursk" set out on its last fatal journey into the cold waters of the Barents Sea. The budgetary constraints on the Russian military caused by the decline of the overall economy meant that the whole complex of equipment, rescue facilities, and morale was inferior to the former Soviet period.

THE SINKING OF THE "KURSK"

In 1992, a few years after the collapse of the Communist regime, but not of the system of naval procurement, the shipyard at Severodvinsk, near to Murmansk on the northern coast of Russia, laid down the hull of what was to become the "Kursk". She was the seventh in a line of powerful submarines in the new class named "Altai" by the Russians, but christened "Oscar- II" class by NATO. Designed by Rubin Central Design Bureau, the class was designed to combat enemy aircraft carrier and other strike-vessel groups with long range, supersonic, anti-ship cruise missiles. They were assigned to the Northern Fleet, Russia's largest. In 1989 K-148 "Krasnodar" had been commissioned; in 1988 K-119 "Voronezh"; in 1990 K-410 "Smolensk"; in1992 K-266 "Oryol"; in1993 K-186 "Omsk"; and on 30th December 1994 K-141 "Kursk" was the latest of these multi-purpose nuclear submarines, to be commissioned.

She was 154 metres long (about the size of two Boeing 747's placed end to end), her beam was 18.2 metres, and her depth, including masts, was 18.3 metres .She weighed 24,000 tons when submerged and she could reach speeds of 32 knots underwater and 16 knots on the surface. She could dive to 600 metres and she could stay submerged for 60 days.

She carried two pressurised water reactors (PWR's) each with a thermal effect of 190 megawatts, or just less than 10% of a typical nuclear power station reactor. She also carried two steam turbines each capable of generating 49,000 shp and two propellers. Her ship's compliment was 107. As one of the latest of the nation's most prestigious pieces of military hardware she also carried the very latest communication, navigation, sonar, and radar equipment.

The "Kursk"s armament capacity was 24 P-700 cruise missiles, called "Granit" by the Russians, but nicknamed "Shipwreck" by NATO, plus 22 torpedoes launched from four 650mm tubes and four 533m tubes. The missiles, which can be launched while a vessel is on the surface or submerged, has a range of 550 kms and travels at 2.5 mach speed. At 10 metres long and weighing seven tons "Shipwreck".

(Dmitry Safronov, the Secret of Kursk's Armaments) can carry both conventional and nuclear warheads. But its chief merit is its unique guidance system. It has, in fact, an "artificial intelligence" electronic system that enables it to strike a specified vessel in a formation. The missile itself selects and classifies the targets by their importance. It can choose its tactic for attack and plan how to carry it out. Its on-board computer is loaded with data on modern classes of ships to enable it to choose appropriate targets. This computer can also counter enemy radio-electronic jamming meant to disrupt its path. The missile is also capable of outwitting missile interceptor's .But even if the "Shipwreck" is hit, due to its huge mass and velocity, it can maintain its initial speed and reach its target. The impact of such a strike is capable of breaking a destroyer-class vessel in two. Two things follow from this: first, when the time came for inspection of the sunken "Kursk", by foreign nationals, the Russian military were extremely edgy about the possible loss of their unique secrets and: when the raising of the vessel was in prospect the divers faced with that task were all too aware of the power of the forces they had to contend with.

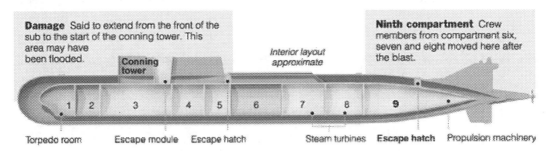

Inside the Kursk New evidence shows that crewmen may have survived in the ninth compartment.

Damage Said to extend from the front of the sub to the start of the conning tower. This area may have been flooded.

Conning tower

Interior layout approximate

Ninth compartment Crew members from compartment six, seven and eight moved here after the blast.

1 2 3 4 5 6 7 8 9

Torpedo room   Escape module   Escape hatch   Steam turbines   Escape hatch   Propulsion machinery

In total there were nine Compartments:

I Missile and torpedo room

II Control room

III Combat station and radio room

IV Living quarters

V Different stations

VI Reactors

VII Main propulsion turbine

VIII Main propulsion turbine

IX Electric motors

Compartments I and IX each had a rescue hatch and on top of Compartment VII was an ascending buoy

For transmitting emergency signals. This buoy, in an emergency such as befell the "Kursk" should have been released automatically by electric signal and floated to the surface. Unfortunately, the "Kursk" emitted neither distress radio signals nor the emergency buoy.

Like its sister vessels the "Kursk" was of double hull construction made of high tensile steel. The outer skin was 8mm thick (just over 1/4 of an inch) with an 80mm thick (about 3

1/4 inches) rubber coat bonded on top to reduce sonar echoes. About 50mm (2inches) of this coating was solid rubber but underneath this was a layer of honeycombed rubber containing small air pockets. (This inner rubber layer was to prove difficult to cut through when the operation to raise the "Kursk" got under way).

The inner pressurised hull was of 50mm (about 2 inches) steel plates. The distance between the two hulls varied between one and two metres. They were connected and reinforced by transverse stiffeners welded to the pressurised and outer hulls. Lodged in the space between the hulls were tools ballast, and equipment of all sorts as well as piping running from bow to stern. (The clearing away of this area proved one of the most difficult and time consuming tasks in the work of preparing the submarine for lifting.)

After being commissioned the `"Kursk" was in active service from 1995 to 2000. In January 1998 it passed an inspection at the Sukhona floating dock in Severodvinsk, where its armament was modernised. In 1999 it appeared on a patrol mission in the Mediterranean. The Americans, alarmed by the presence of such a formidable adversary, put their whole fleet there on full alert. Despite all their efforts, however, they were unable to track it down.

Shortly before what was to prove their submarine's last voyage, the men of the "Kursk "were named as the best crew in the whole Northern Fleet. With that auspicious accolade a recent memory, their vessel began its last voyage at 10am on Thursday 10th August, 2000 under the command of Captain Gennady P. Liachin. Slipping from its mooring in its home port of Vidiayevo in Uraguba Bay, it sailed into the cold waters of the Barents Sea. On board were 118 men; 111 crew, five officers from the 7th SSGN Division Headquarters and two designers.* among them was Senior Lieut Sergei Tylik, in command of the electrical navigation group. Sergei was the son of a submarine captain who, along with his wife, worked in the navy-controlled administration of the town of Vidiayevo. He had wanted to be a submariner since boyhood. He knew his parent's wages were modest and he was willing to accept the bleakness of life on the closed naval garrison at Vidiayevo, with its run down graffiti covered buildings, cut off from the outside world by two checkpoints constantly manned by armed soldiers. Furthermore he was to see the bright and tempting lights of St. Petersburg during his training at the naval college. Yet despite all of this, Sergei still longed to join the service and "go further than his father had done". He married his beautiful wife, Natalya, a nurse, whom he had met at a disco in St. Petersburg during his training, who was prepared to move to Vidiayevo to be with him and their baby daughter, Elizaveta was born there. She was to be her mother and grandparents only solace after the loss of the "Kursk" and its crew. Sergei now had risen to the rank of Senior Lieutenant, probably died in Compartment II. It was his mother who achieved international fame because of her outspoken protests at the meetings of officials and relatives held shortly after the tragedy.

Another crew member was Captain Sergei Dudko, the second in command. He and his wife had two children and Mrs. Dudko was totally dependent on her husband's salary because, as a school librarian, she only earned a modest 1000 roubles (about £25) a month. Captain Dudko's death, probably in Compartment IV, was a devastating blow to his family. Mrs. Dudko later caused uproar by her protests about the conduct of the belated attempts to rescue the crew.

Warrant Officer Oleg Troyan, a technician of the chemical service, probably also died in Compartment IV .His wife, Anna, said later, when officials were considering various options for dealing with the bodies of the submariners, that she would prefer her husband's body to remain entombed in the ill-fated vessel. "I don't want to get a coffin that I'm not allowed to open, that could be filled with stones and rags. I would rather.....throw flowers on the water."

But perhaps the most tragic crew member of all was to be Captain-Lieutenant Dmitry Kolesnikov, aged 27, commander of the technical party for the main propulsion division. When divers recovered his body from Compartment IX of the wrecked submarine his clothes contained the now famous note detailing the survivors last few hours. Olga, a biology teacher, and his wife of only five months, was devastated by the loss of her husband which, she confided later, had changed her life forever.

These were just some of the men, many of them fatalistic, describing the "Kursk" as "an iron coffin", who set out on that mission. They had been ordered to participate in military exercises in the Barents Sea, a mission which one retired Russian admiral, ex-commander of the Black Sea Fleet, Admiral Eduard Baltin, later castigated. He suggested that the subsequent accident was a result of incompetence, bad planning and bad training. "The "Kursk" was designed for the ocean not for shallow waters", he said," Where it was manoeuvring and where it was to perish is completely wild - strong currents and strong winds. You can't carry out torpedo firing there."

On the 12th August at 8:51 Moscow time the "Kursk" sent what was to be her last message, asking for permission to launch her torpedoes against a group of surface ships, lead by the heavy nuclear missile cruiser Petr Velikiy (Peter the Great) positioned some 30 miles from the submarine. She received the response "Dobro" (Good) - then nothing more was heard from her over the communications systems. Gradually Northern Fleet Command realised that something had gone wrong. Peter the Great, and another submarine in the area, had detected two explosions. The "Kursk", we now know, had travelled about 400 metres between the two detonations. But for the people on board the various ships in the area all was silence; frantic efforts to "raise" the "Kursk" were in vain. It was a mystery why none of her sophisticated array of communications facilities had been deployed. At 17:30 Northern Fleet headquarters sent the "Kursk" a radio message-"Report your co-ordinates and operations." No answer. At 23:30 the Fleet Emergency alarm was declared and search forces converged on the area of her last signal. Two Ilushin Il-38's search aircraft reported seeing an oil slick and also emergency buoys and a foreign submarine running at five knots away from the scene. (These latter reports were never confirmed.) The Russian Foreign Ministry also claimed it informed the Norwegians of the accident on the 12th, though as we shall see, the Norwegians had heard only rumours as late as the14th. Late on the 12th the deep sea rescue vessel Mikhail Rudnitsky arrived at the site with two Project 1855 (Priz) submersible rescue craft aboard. It was not until the following day, Sunday the 13th that a sonic depth finder from the Peter the Great located the submarine on the seabed. She was at a depth of 116 metres and heeled over by about two degrees on the port side and five degrees by the bow. The temperature of the water at that depth was three or four degrees Celsius. Shortly afterwards the first two descents to the submarine, from a diving bell from the Mikhail Rudnitsky confirmed her desperate state and reported that there were some feeble knockings from inside the hull. The supposed message was "SOS Water", but this was not decoded until the 18th August when, according to the Russian authorities, it might as likely have been the noise of some machinery. (One US spokesman later claimed that there was no evidence of knocking from the moment the "Kursk" suffered its first explosion.) At seven a.m. on the 13th the Minister of Defence, Igor Sergeyev reported to President Putin on the emergency, but did not recommend his coming to the scene of the tragedy. The President, recently elected and hugely popular after his triumph, was on holiday in the Crimea. His decision not to return to Moscow was to cause him a great deal of unpopularity in the following months. Many citizens were to criticize him openly for not responding more urgently to the crisis. Later, his apologists argued that the President was not given all the facts about the sinking and, therefore, did not know the full extent of it. Certainly there were many senior figures in the navy and the ship building industry who must have feared for their jobs and reputations at the loss of so important a part of the Russian defence capability and the President's absence would have been welcome relief for them. (Mr Putin, in fact, did not arrive back in Moscow until Friday the 18th August.)

Meanwhile Admiral Viacheslav Popov, Commander of the Northern Fleet, had taken command of the rescue efforts from his flagship Peter the Great. Over the following few days 22 vessels and 3000 sailors were to do what they could to rescue any survivors. The submersible rescue vehicles made several attempts to lock onto the rescue hatches but such was the list of the submarine and the deteriorating weather conditions that all such efforts failed. Moreover the Russian authorities rejected early offers of help from other countries. Within Russia itself there was obviously great anxiety and much confusion, especially, among the crew's relatives. They were given assurances that all that could be done were being done. The first word in the press about the rescue operation only appeared on the 15th August, when there was talk of the "active phase" of rescue. On the same day a Remote Observation Vehicle (ROV) inspected the submarine's bow and the public learnt that the two forward Compartments had been flooded. However Commander-in-Chief Vladimir Kuroyedov informed the media that oxygen reserves on the "Kursk" would be sufficient until the 18th. On the 15th the reported knocking stopped. We now know that men from Compartments VI, VII and VIII transferred, soon after the explosions, to Compartment IX. There were 23 of them and at some point there was a fire in that Compartment. The note found on the body of Captain-Lieutenant Kolesnikov tells us that some of the survivors had lived for several hours with a decreasing air supply. It is now believed that the stern Compartment gradually filled with water from leaks in the bulkheads and the stern-tube glands by August the 20th the whole submarine was flooded. On the 17th President Putin evaluated the situation as "critical" and gave his naval commander-in-chief belated orders to accept foreign aid. The public, indeed the whole world, were anxious to know the cause of the disaster. On the 14th Ilya Klebanov, the deputy prime minister assumed control of a government commission to investigate the causes and circumstances of the tragedy. Its first official version of what happened appeared on the evening of the 17th August. The Commission was considering three possible causes:

(1) An external impact, either by collision with a foreign submarine with a minimum displacement of 10,000 tons and moving at a speed of about 10 knots, or with a surface ship, possibly an ice-breaker or ice-strengthened cargo ship, of not less than 150,000 tons. Due to such a collision and the rapid entry of water the "Kursk" would have hit the seabed at sufficient velocity to detonate weapons in the Compartment I. Hence the two recorded seismic events. Under these circumstances most of the crew in all but the last three Compartments would have died in a few minutes. (In a TV interview on the 21st, the Russian Minister of Defence claimed that there were three pieces of corroborative evidence for the "foreign submarine" theory, namely: fragments of a foreign submarine conning tower had been detected 200 metres from the "Kursk" bow; another similar object had been found later; and a foreign buoy had been spotted by one of the Ilyushin planes deployed soon after the search began. None of this evidence was produced later. If such a catastrophic collision had happened it is impossible that the other submarine would have survived.

(1) There was a collision with a foreign submarine.

(2) The "Kursk" had hit a Second World War mine.

(3) There had been "an extraordinary event" in the Compartment I. But the Commission was at pains to make clear that in the case of the torpedoes in the Compartment, these were tried and tested models. The only modification was the replacement of the storage batteries. But, it admitted, there might have been an explosion of hydrogen peroxide. (After further investigation this became the main official version).

The general consensus among Western observers is that during the launch of one of the torpedoes the propellant had first ignited, and then exploded. Within a few minutes one or more warheads had then detonated. It appears that the torpedoes had been upgraded with the solid fuel propellant being replaced by a cheaper, but more dangerous, liquid one. This might explain the presence of the two "designers" -from the Dagdizel military plant - on board.

The Russian officials were above all anxious to convince the world that the submarine had no nuclear weapons on board and that her nuclear reactors had shut down automatically when she sank. They, in fact, issued press releases to this effect. International scepticism was not unnatural at these claims because previous disclaimers had been proved to be false. During all the subsequent rescue and recovery attempts this was to prove one of the disquieting uncertainties in the background. Russia was not renowned as an "open" society and certainly, as other nationals became involved in the operations, there was a lingering doubt about the validity of these claims.

Another explanation surfaced later. A captain on board the Peter the Great, Captain Sergey Ovcharenko, told the Zhizn' newspaper on 31st October 2000 that the cruiser had fired some "Vodopad" ASW rockets contrary to the exercise rules, just at the time of the "Kursk" sinking. He and his friends witnessed a huge explosion and thought that a US submarine had been hit. Only later did they realise that it was the "Kursk" that had suffered damage. This version did not make the running for long - although the divers, who later raised the submarine, were still bandying the story about 12 months later. (Leonid Kharitonov, **Russian Submarine "Kursk" Catastrophe**,)

Assuming that this was the case the vessel would have been deprived of power for heat, lighting, and air purification. The submarine would normally have had back-up batteries to provide power for a limited period but, according to one report, she might have left port without them.

Russian officials had more domestic concerns to deal with. By now the relatives of the crew were becoming a vociferous group, demanding a full explanation of what had gone wrong and what was being done. Mrs Nadezhda Tylik, mother of Sergei Tylik, was beside herself with grief and frustration both at the loss of her son and at the seeming ineptitude of the rescue efforts. In the first instance she had learnt of the accident only from the TV news, just like any other Russian citizen. (She was never to receive an official notification.) There then followed a series of reluctant official disclosures. Eventually it was the outcry of mothers and wives like Mrs Tylik which forced officials, and then the president himself, to meet the relatives face to face. TV footage exists of the first meeting between the relatives and Mr Klebanov on the 18th August. Mrs Tylik's distraught state is there on the screen for all to see as she shouted down the deputy prime minister. The world' audience saw what happened next. She was surrounded by navy personnel and injected, through her clothing, by a nurse who was obviously on stand-by for such an eventuality. It appeared that she had been sedated by force in order to silence her criticisms and the nurse certainly did not seem to ask permission before injecting her. Yet a few days later this seemingly sinister event was explained in quite benign terms by Mrs Tylik. Speaking to a reporter from **The Times** she asserted that as she had a heart condition she had been given an injection of Cardiomin, a heart medication. Her husband, who had been sitting next to her, had seen that she was in a bad state. It was him, said Mrs Tylik, who had held her and called the doctor over. "I really needed that injection", was her explanation. At the moment of Mrs Tylik's collapse the film ended, but she went on to explain what had happened next. "My friend's husband took me out of the hall and I was given a hot cup of tea and some valerian drops. I came back into the hall and I asked our authorities some more questions. I listened to the end and left. I said everything that I wanted to say."

She met Mr Klebanov a few days later and he apologised and said he understood her grief, but he was doing everything in his power. The reporter stated that Mrs Tylik did not appear to be the sort of person who could be pressured into changing her story and when they met she was clear headed and unhesitating.

Mrs Oksana Dudko, wife of one of the "Kursk" captains, also phoned **The Times** reporter and spoke her mind. "Mrs Tylik and Mrs Dudko were not shut up crudely by the authorities. But there is no doubt the Russian Navy would like to smooth over the accident and would prefer these women not to air their views on television," concluded the reporter.

Mr Putin spoke to the relatives for six hours on Tuesday 22nd August. "I have confidence in Mr Putin, "said Mrs Tylik, after meeting him. "He said sorry, though not right away. He has done everything he promised to do," she said .She also praised Admiral Popov, the Commander of the Northern Fleet. "He's a good man. He had the courage to apologise before the women that he could not save their husbands and children," she said.

The Times, Suplement, pp3-4, 29 August, 2000

While all these events occurred in Russia, the rest of the world was slowly becoming aware of the "Kursk" tragedy. In Norway at 9:50 on the 14th August the Norwegian Radiation Protection Authority (NRPA) received a message from the country's Rescue Centre in Bodo, Northern Norway. There were rumours of an accident aboard Russian nuclear submarine the "Kursk". The NRPA declared information preparedness procedures at 10:40 and the Norwegian "crisis committee for nuclear accidents" swung into action. At 13:10 Norway informed the other Nordic countries as well as the International Atomic Energy Agency (IAEA) of the rumours. The crisis committee met that same day and set up a programme for collecting water samples in the accident area. The Norwegians were only too aware that a nuclear submarine lost at such a comparatively shallow depth could cause a major ecological disaster in such productive waters. Nobody, at this stage, could know what would be the environmental consequences of this supposed mishap.

Within a day the Norwegians, indeed the whole world, were aware that the rumoured catastrophe had definitely happened. Several countries, including Norway and Britain, offered help though, as we have seen, this was refused for several crucial days. On the 16th the Russian deputy prime minister announced that there were no longer any signs of life aboard the stricken vessel and, that same day, Britain and Norway were asked for assistance. Such was the degree of concern among other nations that within a few hours of that request a plane carrying the Royal Navy mini-submarine LR5 left Scotland for Trondheim in northern Norway. On the same day the NRPA received its first sea samples gathered by a Norwegian navy vessel some 60 kms west of the sinking. They showed no traces of radioactivity from the "Kursk's" reactors. By the 17th vessels from Norway were on their way to assist in the rescue.

THE FIRST INTERNATIONAL EXPEDITION

On Thursday the 17th August as a supply ship carrying the British LR5 submarine left Trondheim, bound for the "Kursk", the Russians made a further unsuccessful attempt to dock with the submarine. The Russians reported that the entire bow Compartment had been ripped open and that many of the crew who had been there would have died instantly. When operating submerged the crew would have been stationed with **7 men in Compartment I, 36 in Compartment II, 24 in Compartment III, 12 in Compartment IV, 15 in Compartment V, five in Compartment VI, 9 in Compartment VII, 7 in Compartment VIII, and 3 in Compartment IX.** Months later, after the raising of the "Kursk", the Russian Navy's Commander-in Chief, Admiral Vladimir Kuroyedov, told the Interfax News Agency that "the power of the explosion in the first Compartment was so great that machinery and equipment that were in it or the second Compartment were found by divers in the fourth Compartment. Those who know the design of a submarine, where all Compartments are separated by partitions, understand how great the blast really was."

On Friday the 18th August, a Russian rescue capsule briefly locked on to one of the rescue hatches on the submarine. Evidently damage to the hatch itself prevented a successful operation. Obviously a much more sophisticated expedition was necessary. Meanwhile Rubin, the submarine's designers were concluding a contract with the Norwegian company Stolt Offshore to mount an expedition to open the rescue hatch in Compartment IX in an attempt to rescue crew members who might still be alive. On Friday, 18 August Norwegian and British divers went aboard the Dive Support Vessel (DSV) "Seaway Eagle" in Tromso.

The "Seaway Eagle" was mainly employed in the offshore oil industry' was equipped for "saturation diving "(a technique for deep and prolonged Diving), and also carried an ROV. It arrived on site at 8pm on the 19th. During the voyage divers, crew, and managers met in several briefing meetings to discuss the possibility of radiation contamination. It was decided to equip the ROV and the divers with Geiger Muller (GM) monitors for dose rate reading at the working site. The Norwegian, British and Russian parties met on Saturday morning, the 19th. Rear Admiral of the Northern Fleet, Gennady Verich, leading the Russian delegates, described the situation and what assistance the operation required. The meeting's conclusion was that there was no one alive aboard the submarine and that therefore there was no longer any need for the British LR-5, which was never deployed. Later that evening the Russians agreed to allow the ROV to submerge to the seabed for a visual inspection but restricted the inspection to the stern part of the submarine, from the propellers to the reactors Compartment. It was agreed that the divers' main task was to inspect the rescue hatches and the control valve for the inlet/outlet of air in the rescue shaft. There still remained some doubts about whether the Compartment was flooded or whether there was still air inside. Would the divers be faced with possible radioactive contamination if air was released when both hatches were opened? That was the fear. Next morning on Sunday, 20th August, the ROV began its survey of the submarine's stern. The readings of the GM-counter, mounted on the ROV, never exceeded the background level of 0.1 Sv/h. It collected sediment samples on each side of the submarine's hull, as well as water samples. Attempts to open the upper rescue hatches by means of the ROV's hydraulic arms proved unsuccessful.

In preparation for the divers going down to the wreck, on the deck of the Seaway Eagle stood an air sampler to detect any radioactive contamination from air released from the rescue hatch. The divers' self-contained breathing apparatus would prevent the inhalation of radioactive particles and their GM dose rate meters would indicate ambient radiation levels. Readings in the 500-1000 Sieverts Per/hour range would halt the work immediately, (Sievert is a measurement of radiation emitted per hour, the HSE in UK recommend a maximum exposure for a year of 20 micro sieverts) and then a decision, either to terminate the operation or re-schedule the operations, would follow.

On 20th August three Norwegian/British divers made the first descent to the wreck. They believed that the whole vessel was flooded and that any survivors could only be found in possible air pockets in Compartments VII and VIII. They suggested that the air lock would be full of water and might contain the body of a drowned crew member who had attempted to escape. There was obviously considerable tension between the parties on site. Vice-Admiral E. Skorgen, the senior Norwegian officer, who co-ordinated with the Norwegian divers later stated that the Russians had hindered them in their rescue attempts. He told the Nordlandposten newspaper that some of the information provided to the Norwegian divers had compromised their safety. Was this the first evidence of the Russians sensitiveness to outsiders gaining knowledge of their unique weapons' secrets? At this point Admiral Popov intervened so that two Norwegian divers could be flown to another Oscar II submarine to study the hatches and air lock.

On Monday the 21st the divers opened the upper emergency hatch. There were no bodies inside. Later the lower hatch was opened and a large volume of air was released and when this was sampled with the GM counters there were no enhanced levels of radioactivity. Water had completely filled Compartment IX and a video camera on a rod was used to scan inside the Compartment. At this juncture Admirals Popov and Skorgen agreed that everyone on board the vessel had perished. At 21:00 the Military Council of the Northern Fleet officially announced the loss of all hands and expressed its condolences to all the relatives. August 23rd was pronounced a day of national mourning. On the 22nd Igor Sergeyev, Minister of Defence, Vladimir Kuroyedov' Navy Commander-in-Chief, and Admiral Popov handed in their resignations. President Putin would not accept them but rather ominously stated that his refusal did not absolve anyone from possible responsibility.

It was at this stage that Admiral Popov asked the Norwegian divers if they would assist in finding and bringing out any of the casualties. Because this was a departure from the plan for the expedition Stolt Offshore were contacted. Subsequently, on the morning of Tuesday 22nd, all parties agreed that the expedition's original objectives had been achieved, the hatch in Compartment IX was battened down, and by 15:00 most of the Norwegians were on their way to Kirkenes by helicopter. Thus ended the first international expedition to the "Kursk".

THE "MSV REGALIA" EXPEDITION

With the" Seaway Eagle" expedition completed the Russians now sought a way of recovering the bodies of the casualties. In Russia itself, among both relatives and public alike, this recovery was essential. President Putin's loss of credibility in his handling of the crisis would be partly restored if all efforts were focussed on this operation. . As well as the recovery of the bodies there would be the opportunity to trace documents and instruments on board in order to verify the definitive reasons for the catastrophe. During September 2000 Russian authorities again officially applied to Norway for assistance. The subsequent Support Vessel "Regalia" expedition lasted from 20th October to 7th November.

The" Regalia" was a platform-like vessel especially suited to diving activities in the North Sea. The Norwegian/US firm of Halliburton secured the contract, worth some $5.8 million, at a very late stage - only three weeks before the 20th October. There was little time for preparations by both sides. Halliburton employees visited Russia to discuss with specialists the best places to cut into the "Kursk's" hull. For their part Russian divers joined the Regalia in Bergen before it sailed so that during the ten day voyage they and the Halliburton crew could do some test diving, training routines and equipment checks. The intention was to retrieve the dead crew members through eight apertures cut in the hulls by foreign and Russian divers. Only 25 to 35 bodies were expected to be found.

It became evident that the Russians did not have the necessary equipment for ""saturation diving" necessary for this "Kursk" project. The divers on the "Kursk" would have to work at a pressure of 10 atmospheres and to stay in the small, six person, saturation chambers during the three to four weeks of the operation. Eighteen divers from Russia, Norway, and GB worked on the job, but after an early decision, only Russian divers would enter the submarine while the others were responsible for cutting the access holes. Halliburton, in short, was in charge of diving safety, all equipment and the cutting of the holes. The Russian Northern Fleet and the Rubin Company, who were the submarines designers, were the clients and they determined where the holes should be cut. Eight Compartments were to be cut into. Again, as on the "Seaway Eagle" expedition, there was concern about possible radiation dangers and the leakage of radioactivity from the submarine. Once more, experts drew up proper procedures for sampling, dose rate measurements and proper protection. As on the "Seaway Eagle" if the dose rate rose to unacceptable levels the dive was to stop and further assessments would be made. As also on the previous expedition both the ROV and the divers would carry the necessary monitors.

On the 20th October the vessel stopped close to the "Kursk" site and the divers did some test diving? One feature of the "Regalia" was the production of its own drinking water by distilling seawater, but at this point the intake was stopped for fear of drawing in contaminated water. The vessel could manage for several days without taking in further seawater. When the ROV went down to survey the submarine it gathered water and sediment samples. Once these were analysed and found to be free of dangerous radiation freshwater production started up again.

This time the ROV was allowed to survey the bow of the "Kursk". The scene was one of devastation. The whole bow Compartment had been blasted apart, with two large cracks running further along the hull as far as the conning tower, with smaller cracks evident further back. In all, about 18 meters of the submarine was a tangled mess, with wreckage strewn around. Among the debris were several pieces from torpedoes, and these were removed.

Divers first went down on Friday night, the 20th October and on the "Saturday morning to work on Compartment VIII. Once the outer hull had been breached, their first job was to depressurise tubes between the hulls: tubes that might have been at 400 bar pressure. Thereafter the cutting started using a circular and linear device pumping high pressure water containing specially imported grit through a 2mm nozzle. Like the later and larger expedition, which raised the "Kursk", these divers had difficulty cutting through the rubber outer layer of the vessel. When the Russian divers eventually entered the submarine they caused consternation among the other divers by refusing to wear their GM dose meters. They contended that these impeded movement. To get round this possible hazard someone would lower a meter to them so they could take readings and these were relayed to divers outside.

Over the next few days, the men cut out various pieces of the inner and outer hulls and these were lifted to the" Regalia". At three pm on the 25th Midshipman Sergei Shmyrdin was the first person to enter Compartment VIII. The visibility was good and there were no signs of a fire. The divers then opened the hatch leading to Compartment IX, but immediately the dust and ashes inside it made visibility poor. However they were able to open the rescue hatch in the Compartment and a camera was lowered to them. There were no casualties in the Compartment's first floor, but on the next floor down they found the first body and it was lifted out of the submarine by rope. A little later they found two more and these were also taken out. These three victims showed clear signs of having been badly burnt. Later that day a fresh Russian team found two more casualties in this, the rearmost compartment.

Next morning the Russian Admiral told an information meeting that all the bodies had been examined by specialists. One of the victims, Lieutenant Kolnikov, carried a note the poignancy of which was to echo around the world. He said he was writing by touch because of the complete darkness in Compartment IX, to where he and his comrades from Compartments VI, VII, and VIII had retreated. There were 23 of them. He sent his love to his wife but said he did not think they had a better than 20% chance of surviving. Sergei Kolnikov made several separate entries over, what must have been, several hours, but gradually hypothermia and carbon dioxide poisoning must have extinguished the lives of these desperate men sealed in "the iron coffin" in horrendous conditions. The note contained information important for solving the question of why the "Kursk" sank. Consequently cutting in Compartment VII stopped and more holes were cut in Compartment IX to provide better access for retrieving more bodies.

On Saturday 28th October a Russian helicopter took the bodies to Murmansk and later that day a new Russian diving team found the sixth casualty as well as documents, oxygen masks, a survival suit and a bag. Later still they found four more casualties, not all of whom showed signs of having been burnt. On Sunday two more casualties brought the number to twelve and these were the last to be discovered on this expedition.

Meanwhile a piece had been cut from the conning tower and taken to the surface for examination. Then Compartment III, the combat station and radio room, was cut into and closer inspection of the inner hull piece showed that there had been a very active fire in that Compartment.   Cables, ashes and debris were strewn everywhere and as access was impossible the divers screwed the cut section back into the hole.

Compartment IV, the living quarters, showed no signs of fire and visibility in it was good. There were no casualties inside the Compartment but the divers collected debris and documents from the command section

On Sunday, 5th November divers cut pieces of the bow Compartment and they were lifted on the deck of the "Regalia" The expedition finished with further sediment samples being taken from either side of the submarine and then all personnel held a commemorative service on the main deck of the "Regalia" in the presence of an admiral from the Northern Fleet.

On both the "Seaway Eagle" and "Regalia" expeditions all the divers used personal dosimeters (about 4 ½ inches square) from the National Radiation Protection Board (the British NRPB). Divers wore them under their diving suits while in the water. When not diving they were handed to the diving supervisor until the next dive. These procedures became routine where there is a possibility of exposure to elevated levels of radiation. The dosimeters are not protection devices but do show the total dose received during a set period. After the "Seaway Eagle" expedition four of the six divers were below the detection limit of exposure but two were above. Results after the "Regalia" project showed that all divers were below the detection limit.

During the latter expedition a personal dosimeter from one of the casualties, which the Russians claimed belonged to a worker from the reactor Compartment, number VI, showed only background levels of radiation. As found elsewhere in the Barents Sea. In short, on both expeditions all dose rate measurements gathered by the ROV's showed normal background levels of radiation and no evidence of radiation leakage from the submarine. Similar results came from the sediment analyses.   There was no evidence of the enhanced presence of radionuclide's, in the surrounding area due to leaks from the submarine. The levels found were similar to concentrations normally found in the sea.

However, the report "The Kursk Accident" from the NRPA, written in June 2001, before the successful attempt to raise the "Kursk" had started, still left room for concern for the future - and for future expeditions. Uncertainties abounded about the continuing state of the reactors - the types of radionuclide present and their activity level; about the rate of release of radionuclide over time; about the absorption and transport of different radionuclide in the currents at the seabed. So for those who were to be involved in the monumental task of preparing the "Kursk" for lifting and for seeing that operation through, all these variables and uncertainties were present in the depths of the Barents Sea?

The Resolve to Raise the "Kursk"

President Putin had suffered a great loss of popularity from his mishandling of the crisis. When the "Komsomolets", another submarine designed by Rubin, sank in April 1989 the general public and even the families and staff at its home base had remained silent. The atmosphere of secrecy, of lack of communication and information under the old regime still held Russians in thrall. When the "Kursk" sank things were different. The climate of glasnost, of "openness" had begun to alter the willingness of people to accept what they were told to accept. Also this was such a major calamity, the largest submarine loss in Russian history, that now people was prepared to criticise and question. The deaths of 118 men and the bungled rescue attempts were too much for the Russian people to stomach.

President Putin quickly learnt that only the recovery of the submarine, or at least the bodies of the victims would "satisfy his nation. Thus he resolved to raise the 26,000 ton "Kursk" from the seabed and with it thus recovers the remaining corpses. Some cynical observers were convinced that the main reason for the raising of the vessel had less to with reclaiming the dead but much to do with retrieving the Granite missiles and all the research and development which they had entailed. Deputy Prime Minister, Ilya Klebanov had earlier said "No single country on its own can handle such an operation". Indeed shortly after the tragedy Russia and the Netherlands established the "Kursk Foundation" in order to meet some of the enormous costs of the project of the raising, estimated between £70 million and £100 million, and thus avert an ecological disaster. But lifting the "Kursk" off the seabed was only one option being considered early on. Admittedly it headed the list of options either by lifting with cables attached to a platform, which is what happened eventually, or by using giant air cushions strapped to the hull. (Paul Beaver of Jane's Information Group was just one of those who had speculated that this was a feasible venture in the relatively shallow depths of the Barents Sea). Some said such an operation could not be rushed. Nils Bohmer, of the Bellona Foundation based in Oslo, warned in August 2000 that even if the submarine spent a winter on the seabed it would be better to wait until the summer of 2001 before attempting the lift. He maintained that it normally took at least three months for a submarine's nuclear reactors to cool down and any attempt to move the vessel too soon would crack the hull, releasing radioactive material into the sea.

Others argued for different solutions. Some experts said the "Kursk" was too damaged to withstand the lifting operation that it should be sawn in pieces and each Compartment raised separately. Some wanted only the reactors raised, although this option would require very special and expensive equipment. Still others thought that dragging the submarine to shallower water would solve the problem, at least temporarily. In that case the bodies could be removed more easily. But critics answered that this was still a dangerous undertaking. Still another idea was to seal off the reactors and leave the vessel on the seabed. In fact the Russians had developed a special biological gel which is said to seal all cracks and is lighter than conventional materials. Though expensive, the Russians claimed it would last 500 years. When the "Komsomlets" sank in 1989 they had used this method and, as already noted, at least some of the relatives would have preferred the bodies to rest in peace. All the previous lost nuclear submarines had been left where they lay - though in very different situations from the "Kursk".

In December 2000 the former Russian Minister of Foreign Affairs, Alexander Bessmermykh and former Netherlands Defence Minister William van Eckelen, co-chairmen of the "Kursk Foundation" called a meeting of its top executives in Brussels to present their plans to hoist the "Kursk" to the surface. On hand was Igor Spassky, a vice chairman of the Fund and director of the Rubin Central Design Bureau (CKB), the "Kursk's" designers. At a press conference the Fund's leaders summarised the three months work of experts from Russia, Norway, the UK, Sweden, Italy and other countries, while experts spoke about different aspects of the lifting operation.

Academician Spassky had said earlier that a contract between Rubin and an international salvage consortium must be signed about the beginning of February 2001 so that the work could be completed by September. Negotiating contractors included the US firm Halliburton and two Dutch companies - Smit International and Heerema. Klebanov estimated the contract as worth about £70 million. The International Fund was ready to shoulder half the costs, but would only start raising the money after the contract was signed. Foreign minister Ogor Ivanov on a visit to Holland made a statement declaring that Moscow does not want financial assistance in the Kursk operation linked by the west "with issues not directly related to the salvage operation" Moscow means the leading European Union countries to include financial aspects of the salvage operation in the global program of Northern seas "nuclear decontamination". The Kremlin must have perceived it as an attempt to intervene in Russia's domestic affairs. According to Ivanov Russia would finance the operation itself if the West insisted on any additional conditions with regard the Kursk? If this was the case, the salvage operation may be postponed for a year. The government's directive on the salvage, transportation, and placement of the nuclear submarine Kursk into a floating dock which Prime Minister Mikhail Kasianov signed recently does not allocate sufficient sums to the operation, whose costs estimated at about $80 million. The document orders the Finance Ministry to allocate 500 million roubles from the April-July budget 2001 for the restoration of technical readiness of the ships to be directly involved in the operation. Along with that, in April – May the Finance Ministry and Defence Ministry are supposed to find financial sources for the purchase of equipment and gear to the value of 900 million roubles. All this falls far short of Klebanov's $80 million estimate. The rest of the money was to be raised by the International Kursk Foundation. The possibility of rejection of the financial assistance from the west is broached in the document diplomatically. It states "If the International Kursk Foundation fails to raise the necessary sum" the Finance Ministry and

Defence Ministry "are to forward their proposals to the cabinet on additional sources funding in 2001 and 2002." Meaning, postponement for a year.

Negotiations continued throughout the winter and spring 2000/2001. President Putin was anxious to conclude the operation by September in order to placate Russian public opinion. Eventually Smit and Halliburton declared that the scheme was not feasible in that time scale and the project looked to be in jeopardy. Unexpectedly, however, another Dutch firm - Mammoet - experienced in heavy lifting and transporting of loads in the oil industry, stepped in. Mammoet, which had no experience of lifting from the seabed such heavy loads as the "Kursk", offered a lower price and guaranteed the work would be completed in 2001. Mammoet quoted £43 million. Once successful in the bidding, Mammoet immediately joined in negotiations with Smit and then Halliburton so that all three companies could pool their expertise to ensure a successful operation. And so, by May 2001, the plan existed to recover the "Kursk". This envisaged the building, in the Netherlands, of a huge barge, the Giant 4, with 26 "Grabber" cables. This would be sailed into the northern ocean and positioned over the stricken submarine. The operation involved firstly cutting off the damaged front end of the vessel and then a team of 30 divers (British, Norwegian and Russian) would accurately drill 26 holes in the submarines hull. The 26 cables could then be attached and, weather permitting; the hull could be hoisted to lie underneath the barge for towing slowly to the dry dock in Murmansk.

Despite these credentials and the apparent confidence of those involved, there is no doubt that this imaginative scheme was fraught with hazards. Would the submarine leak radioactive material during the operation and, more especially during the lift? Would any of the torpedoes left in the front Compartment explode during the cutting? Could the truncated submarine be lifted intact and withstand the journey to its destination? The divers must have contemplated all these problems, and more, as they became aware of their involvement. At this time I was working for British Petroleum North Sea in May and June unaware I was to become one of the four diving supervisors, and my responsibilities were to be especially onerous. I had 20 years experience in the diving field, both as an air and "saturation diver and as a diving supervisor but I knew that nothing as large as the "Kursk" had ever been lifted before, especially not from such a depth. This operation was the equivalent of lifting a Second World War battleship from the ocean floor. The trials and strains on both manpower and equipment in the following few months were to be unique in the annals of deep sea salvage operations.

SATURATION DIVING TECHNIQUES

The depth of water the Kursk is resting in is 116metres the diving techniques required for this salvage operation will be Saturation. This technique requires the divers to be compressed in chambers to the equivalent depth. Physics tells us the pressure the atmosphere exerts on the human body is 14.7 Ibs per square inch on the surface at 116metres it will be more than 10 times this pressure the divers will experience during this operation. The breathing medium will not be air as the nitrogen in the air is narcotic at depth, we substitute the nitrogen with helium which only side effect is you speak like Donald duck and communication is a little harder. When the body is subjected to these conditions the body absorbs the gas at the increased pressure it finds it self at. When the diver returns to the surface he will be ascend at a calculated rate so the body can vent of this extra gas through the lungs during the exhale when breathing. If the ascent is to quick, as the gas expands in the body and if can not be vented off through breathing this can cause decompression sickness which can manifest itself as pain or neurological problems which can be mild or in some cases paralysis and death, the media often refer to this condition as the Bends. When the body absorbs this extra gas it will keep on absorbing while at that depth but after 6 hours the body can absorb no more, the body has become saturated hence the diving technique is called **Saturation**. After six hours the time it takes to return to the surface is the same for six hours or six weeks. With this information we can keep divers at that depth for indefinite periods if we wanted to, the law in U.k. stipulates the divers can remain in saturation for a maximum of 28 days which will include the decompression and for this depth it will be 4 days 17 hours 7 minutes. Where the divers live during this period is called the Sat System, on the Mayo the vessel she will be participating in the salvage, has 2 main chambers which can house six men each, a decompression chamber which can hold six for decompression requirements, in addition to this we have two bells which lock on and off the system these transport the divers from the DSV(Dive Support Vessel) to the Kursk at 116 metres, where they will work for a maximum of six hours then be returned to the DSV saturation system for their rest period. There will be four working teams of three divers in the system at all times more during periods of decompression, but with four teams the rest period is usually 14 to 16 hours. When the divers are in the system they will require feeding, ablutions, laundry and all the normal requirements a person needs to live. The chambers are equipped toilets, showers, sinks. All other requirements such as food and laundry is passed back and forth through locks in the system which when used correctly contain its integrity. This system is maintained by the unsung heroes of diving, the mechanical and electrical technicians and the LST's(Life Support Technicians) these people take care of the divers 24 hours a day 7 days a week 365 days a year. They also ensure the correct mixture of gas is use and control any decompressions that maybe required. A deck crew is also very important they lock the bells on and off, send down and recover the equipment required by the divers to perform the tasks asked of them. There are a lot of people required to keep two divers working on the submarine at any one time. A saturation diver is a strange breed of person, he must not suffer from claustrophobia no even a little bit because living in a chamber with 5 other guys for up to 4 weeks will bring it to the fore, he must get on with his colleagues you can not fall out with someone and carry on living in such close proximity without someone losing it, they must have courage to do this kind of work and madness helps. For the divers who may read this book I have tried to keep the description of sat diving for the layman and refrained from mentioning excursions, gas partial pressures, storage depths, trying to keep the technical side to a minimum.

THE SALVAGE

The contract for the project was signed on 18th May.   On the 21st May Mammoet and Smit announced that they had agreed on a joint venture to raise the "Kursk". Smit would be responsible for converting a heavy lift barge for the lifting phase. There was a proviso in the contract that those who had signed it would be released from their obligations if bad weather intervened.

On the 23rd May, just a few days after the contract had been agreed, I made my first entry in which I am sure will become a daily ritual, hopefully I am recording history with a successful conclusion each entry will convey my thoughts on that day at that time irrespective of what is happening outside my knowledge, when I am on the job I expect to have little or no contact with the outside media, "*to-day was the first time we (ships crew) had heard anything to do with the "Kursk" job. Out of the blue we were told that there were rumours that we might be involved. I wasn't quite sure what it would involve but this started us all buzzing a bit* "

On the 25th "*we heard the first announcements to confirm …. There will be a salvage operation. The Russian…… President Putin made an announcement the Russian Federation are going to recover the "Kursk" from the Barents Sea and will be lifted on the 20th September.*"

On the same day; on the internet , came a report that Russian Navy senior officers as well as senior Kremlin officials had admitted for the first time that there were dangers inherent in the lifting operation because the vessel still carried functioning torpedoes and cruise missiles. "A naval officer (Navy Commander Vladimer Kuroyedov) told journalists that it was possible that at least one torpedo might go off during the operations to cut off the forward part of the wreck. Indeed Deputy Prime Minister Klebanov went further and conceded that "salvage experts could not give a 100% guarantee that the nuclear reactors would not leak once the "Kursk" was lifted off the seabed." He added that Russia would accept the responsibility for any such leaks.

At the same time Sergei Yastrzhembski, President Putin's media co-ordinator, said that Russia wished to make the operation a model of multi-media openness. To that end the authorities would open a web-site for constant updating of the procedures. By the 27th we were aware of what had been said - "they *expect one of the torpedoes to go off during the recovery bloody hell*".

By the 28th May all was uncertainty. *"It has gone very quiet (concerning the "Kursk" project) apart from various rumours that we have got it, other contradictory rumours claimed that we haven't".*

On the afternoon of the 8th of June. *"Had a bit of good news as far as the "Kursk" job is concerned. As I was leaving the vessel to go home for some time off, I asked Wally (dive superintendent my boss) if he had any word on the Kursk project, he said "I can't tell you anything just yet its still top secret all I can say is **go get a woolly hat** its going to be cold where we are going next, and you will need it in about 10 days". I took that as a subtle hint we have the job, but we....couldn't announce it yet because of the security involved."* Ten days later on the 18th June: *"the biggest scoop to date I suppose on the "Kursk" a theory I've heard of what actually happened to this submarine, and why it sunk. Whereas they have told everyone that it was a collision sub-sea or the Americans had attacked or banged into them, and the theory of an on-board explosion has been put to one side. The latest is, part of their war games exercise was for one of their destroyers to fire a bombardment of shells into the area where the "Kursk" was supposed to be. After one hour, the "Kursk" would then surface and return fire and simulate the sinking of the destroyer. Apparently, the destroyer was an hour late when it fired its salvo, it was at the same time as the submarine came to the surface and one of the shells hit the nose of the submarine and it sank. The only confirmation we have of this is from a fellow diver who was on one of the previous trips up there on the "Regalia", he informed one of our divers there was nothing left of the nose., it's not just this crack down the side as they had told us all along; He reckons it's blown to Smithereens and it's all over the place, there's not much of it left. Which fits with the destroyer theory?*

On the very next day the proflowers.com website (USA today) reported what was to be one of the diver's worst nightmares - that the "Kursk" had been carrying nuclear devices. Grigory Tomchin, a member of the Russian government's investigating commission, had confirmed as much in a TV interview with Norway's TV-2. "That this information has been known for a long time," he told the TV audience. Tonchin, who was also a Russian lawmaker, went on to say he "was tired of all the secrecy about the wreck" and encouraged the military to be more open.

In corroboration of this alarming statement "Harold Ramfjord, a Norwegian engineer who had been central in planning the proposed salvage of the "Kursk", said he also had seen secret Russian documents confirming the presence of atomic weapons. "One of the documents I had access too said there were two atomic missiles on board and that was stamped "secret" said Ramfjord who worked for the Global Tool Management offshore oil industry group. For himself he made it clear he would not proceed with the salvage operation if the missiles were still on board. TV - 2 said that NATO called the SSN - 19 missiles "Shipwrecks". They each had 500 kiloton nuclear warheads.

On that same day I was oblivious of what been said in Norway, and was still preparing for the project. "The salvage team expect us now to start around about the 3rd of July with a three day mobilisation and then sail for Russia which will take seven day of steaming. Incorporated in the transit would be some training dives for the Russian divers, we can check out their skills and they can familiarise themselves with our equipment.....We believe the Russian divers have been all over the sister ship (or boat as submarines are called), getting to know their way around it, which is obviously a big advantage for them . The British divers are going to get straight into cutting the holes while the Russian divers will be responsible for the marking it up of the locations where the outer sections are to be removed and the pressure hull locations for the holes. Then at a later date we will remove the forward Compartment and rig up for recovery. Sounds quite an easy task, if you say it fast.

"There is a lot of ordering of equipment as you would expect on a job like this. Endless lists are being put together for equipment to last us for an indefinite period. We don't have any information about crew changes, supplies of gas, etc. that you need on long jobs like this. We do have a backup plan of what we will need from a diving point of view. What we require for the work we can only guesstimate as best and order what we think we will need plus 10% for good luck. I suspect we will stuff the ship full of everything we can. The last thing we want is to be caught without something we had not thought of.

20th JUNE

Received some more information today.....the reason they have to cut the front Compartment off is that they only have 1 metre clearance between the Dry Dock (where the "Kursk" will be taken) and the barge + submarine. If the nose was not removed and dropped down they would be in trouble. They won't have the clearance they need to get it into the Dry Dock it would obstruct the entrance that would leave them a barge with a submarine underneath and nowhere to put it. We're going to go into the front Compartment first with a jet prop (this is a machine that forces a water jet downwards) to clear the silt and debris. They need to know the locations of the unaccounted torpedoes and what state they are in. Once located we need to know, whether we have to move or defuse them. That's another task that's going to be a bit dodgy.

Right now, the Russians divers are in Murmansk Navel Base diving on the sister ships outer hull familiarising themselves, they will be responsible for marking up the submarine on the outer hull which sections have to be removed for access to the inner pressure hull where the lifting holes are to be made. This has to be very accurate because these holes will have to line up with the same holes being fabricated on the lifting barge in Holland.

"The Russians are coming over with 20 personnel. Four of them are divers, two are supervisors, there are submarine experts and four more described as "others" I don't know who they can be. They are coming early so hopefully there will be some team bonding which is imperative for this type of work. We are going to take all the gas for this job with us, the cutting and jet prop equipment will be supplied by Mammoet / Smit it will be a very full vessel when we sail. We sail in about 2 day's time and on the way we are going to do some trials with the divers.

When we get to the accident site we are going to position the vessel over the submarine and deploy the radioactive sonar array to monitor for any radioactivity. This has previously been deployed when the other vessels, "Seaway Eagle" and "Regalia" visited earlier. When we're happy with the findings, we can go ahead and dive. We intend to go straight into the hull in the forward Compartment.

We have permission to send a couple of diving representatives across to Russia shortly to have a look at the sister ship. Hopefully try and get some photographs and video footage for us - but it's all very secretive now. Whether the Russians will let us or not were not sure yet.

"The insurance is still a sticking point but apparently for the divers and other personnel it is already in place; it's for the vessels. Obviously the vessels are worth a lot more than a few scabby old divers. The project looks like over a hundred days long and they are being generous with the time schedule for the tasks that we have to do, which is the opposite when you are working in the commercial industry. They always seem to give you as little time as possible for the job. We've also been instructed that there are to be no Brits going into the submarine; if there is any intervention work to do inside it must be Russian.

21ˢᵗ JUNE

Well, the "Kursk" job seems to be becoming more urgent by the day. They are bringing it forward all the time and are now saying we have to mobilise on the 26th because the time scale is all important. The superintendents still hope to be going to Russia to see the sister ship/submarine. We have been able to ask a few questions here and there. We're not sure of the replies. We don't know the state of the ordnance on board. That's one of the jobs we're going to have to do first.

What are they going to pay us? .... It looks like there will be no danger money for this job, they expect us to do all this work while sitting over nuclear reactors, intercontinental ballistic missiles all in an unknown state of stability the company do not class it as dangerous. So there has been no mention of any danger money or anything remotely indicating extra money will be forthcoming. I think there are a few divers who might want a bit more. I don't blame them and a few extra quid would not go amiss for me either.

23ʳᵈ of JUNE

"I've had a meeting with my boss, an informal meeting, about what's happening. It looks like now I'm going to be called back on the 2nd. I leave the boat today, so I'll get a week at home. On the 3rd all the Russians are coming over. They're going to have enough people onboard to pair people off with a Russian. Each man will then show his respective partner around the boat and familiarise him with the vessel. We will show them the work stations where they will be assisting the divers. We will also show them the "saturation system and will give them a chance to familiarises themselves with it. In effect it will be a case of chaperoning the Russian divers around until they are happy. We touched on the length of trip and it looks like it will be six weeks for me anyway with a two week break. The Russians are expected to do the full trip however long it will be.

I've just been asked if I want to go, over to Holland to do the risk assessments on the 2nd July.... I said yes, it would be quite interesting to see how you risk assess nuclear reactors, torpedoes, and intercontinental ballistic missiles.

Meanwhile on the 29th June far away in the Alexander Hotel on Bolshaya Yakmanka Street in Moscow, the destinies and work patterns for my colleagues and I were being decided at the highest level. An august assembly met at the hotel under the auspices of various agencies including the National Information Service Kursk Strana Ru, set up in accordance with the Russians promise to keep the world informed of developments. The press conference intended to answer journalists' questions from the floor as well as those from internet users on the conference website. In attendance were the Deputy Commander - in Chief of the Russian Navy, Vice Admiral Mikhail Barskov, Chief of Naval Press Service, Igor Dygalo, Franz Van Seumeren President of the Mammoet Company and Hans Van Rooy Director of the Smit Company. First to address the conference was Van Seumeren who said that Mammoet had, in the past, been involved in some very large jobs including lifting the roof onto the Olympic Stadium in Moscow where they had used the same strength jacks as they intended to use on the "Kursk". He also explained that in the off-shore field they often had to move big modules on barges. The Russian company Sevinash were subcontracted to do a good deal of work on modifications and the Krylov Institute is subcontracted to assist also. Mr. Van Seumeren admitted that the "Kursk" project was a very delicate and challenging job for his firm. The huge barge, at the moment in Amsterdam, would eventually arrive on site and lift the submarine. Everything was proceeding normally, he said and he was "fully "satisfied" with the mutual relationships they had developed with Rubin - "they are very high level professionals". Next week the ships would leave for the site. "Initially we will undertake the necessary investigations of the hull". On approximately 16th July an additional pontoon equipped with specialised ventilation devices will set out from Rotterdam and in late August or September the huge barge will sail from Amsterdam. Around 10th September they would start the connection of the cables and the lift should be between the 15th and 20th September. "You must understand that we are working a very complicated timetable, because the period between the signing of the contract and the works themselves is very small." "We have solved all the technical problems and we hope that the weather will be decent."

Vice -Admiral Boskov confirmed that firms within Russia were doing experimental work on the grappling devices and were checking every aspect of safety - something that we would find frustrating later on. Barskov also gave details of the work of the 23 ships posted to the area. Some would guard the area, others would permanently monitor for radiation, and others would be delivering technological equipment. He confirmed that no divers would be involved in, nor indeed near the area of, the cutting off of the first Compartment. "Everything will be done by remotely from the surface, he explained. "As regards Granit missiles, I must tell you they are absolutely safe. All of them are in containers, which are as strong as the sub's solid hull. They will be removed from the submarine after it is placed in dock." Rubin, he said, had had a "big Meeting" with many European experts, the "main one of them was from Britain. He is the chief radiation expert of the British Navy. He said literally this - our (the Russian) security requirements are far greater than we (the British) have in the Royal Navy."

Admiral Barskov then answered a question from the German magazine **"Stern "**. What do you know about how many unexploded torpedoes still remain in the first Compartment, and how many of them are training torpedoes and how many combat torpedoes?" To this Barskov replied: "the overall TNT equivalent of the charges in the first Compartment before the accident was approximately 10 tons. After the explosion we consider it still holds several warheads from torpedoes that did not detonate."

Then Hans Van Nooij faced a question. What kind of access would film crews have for covering the lifting operation? asked a Norwegian journalist. Van Nooij replied that during the operation they would try to provide safety for the journalists, though," actually this place will not be accessible to the media." There would be press conferences and visits at odd times though the main information would go via the Internet. Igor Dygalo then added: "we will seek to ensure an equal access to information and..... the maximum level of openness,"

On the surface then all seemed certain and assured but as we were to discover very soon, all was not as watertight on the safety side as it appeared.

I am Unaware of the goings on at the Alexander Hotel, on the same day I noted " *the destination of Holland has changed....for the risk assessment it has been relocated to Aberdeen, it's starting to hit home now , we're going to do this, and it's going to be a very dangerous job..."*

By the 2nd July I was aware of the Moscow press conference which, as I saw it, was rather one-sided. *"I'm at home, and I've just been reading the press release that was on the Internet from the "Kursk" website.... They had all the top boys there at the meeting..... They say some interesting things......they don't mention the British divers and they are alluding to the fact that the Russians are going to do all the work and the "foreign divers "as we are known, (and implying that we are Dutch and Norwegian, which we are obviously not) will be in the bell, while the Russians go out and do all the work!!! In reality you will find that we will do all the work, we have the expertise, unfortunately the Russians do not. It's interesting that they are not mentioning that there are British divers involved but I think it's all to do with secrecy, and they don't want the so-called super powers of America and Great Britain (if you can call Great Britain super powers) to be seen to be helping the Russians. They want to give the impression that their boys are doing it with the aid of Dutch and Norwegian experts in lifting. They do mention which ship is going - the "Mayo", which is the correct ship at least. It belongs to DSND, a Norwegian company, so it looks as if they are using the neutral Norwegians.*

The consortium of the Russian and Dutch are going to keep a very strict control over the media. They will not be letting them on the Kursk site. A press co-ordination site will be established and all information will be channelled through it. The media are claiming that they need to visit the wreck site and interview the crew, I would be very surprised if they allow the media anywhere the site let alone interview us . They may get a flying visit for the pretext of openness of the salvage operation, but I am sure they would not let them interview us.

3rd JULY

I've just arrived on the vessel in Aberdeen and dumped my gear in my cabin; quite a lot has been going on. We've moved a lot of the equipment off the deck to make room for the stuff we're taking with us. As you can imagine, it's chaos on here. Bed space is at a premium. People are roaming the corridors wondering where they are going to sleep tonight; I've got a bed so I'm OK. It's merely the logistics going on right now, mainly who is sleeping where. The Russians have arrived in Aberdeen and will be quarantined in a hotel away from the press for the night.

Tomorrow we're going to start the risk assessment, which maybe will last two days....which is Wednesday 4th and we're still looking at sailing on Friday 6th. We have some trials to conduct on the sail over to Norway, checking equipment and the dive system. It's quite hectic right now - people coming and going, welders securing vast amount of equipment into position for the sail. There seem to be 101 things to do before we can sail.

4th JULY

"Well, what a morning it's been so far. On the quayside we've got a media circus - cameras and videos ready to record the arrival of the Russians. Apparently they have been following them around ever since they arrived in the UK. In Aberdeen they had five full media crews tracking them down. But now the media attention is poised at the bottom of the gangplank waiting for them to join the vessel today.

Its half past six in the evening I have just returned from our first day of Risk assessing." A lot of the questions we put forward can't be answered because there is nobody here with the expertise or knowledge to answer them. With no answers forthcoming our only course of action left to us is to record our questions and give them to the Russians who will on pass to those who can answer them, this leaves our risk assessment with a lot of actions on the Russian federation. I was sitting next to the Russian entourage and I questioned the navel officer next to me about the lack of information supplied by them .He shrugged his shoulders and said he had did not think they should be here anyway, I think the concept of risk assessment was alien to him, they did leave shortly after. We continued with the generic tasks were going to employ these tasks are not new to us and performed them many times in the past. Now we have covered all the tasks that we can cover, we are really getting down to the nuts and bolts of the job now and the input from the Russians is critical things like armaments, nuclear reactors and torpedo's. It's a bit frustrating right now with the only answers we get from them is "we will refer that question to the Russian Federation. Hopefully tomorrow we will get some co-operation, which is severely lacking to-day.

The Russians are on board now, their embarking was all primed for the best media reaction possible .At this moment in time they are exploring the vessel in there brand new blue overalls, while the media on the quayside are videoing any glimpses of them they can. There has been plenty of media attention to-day and some of our crew have been videoed doing our every day tasks making us into film stars of the future no doubt. The intention is to go ashore to-night and start some team bonding with Russian divers a few drinks will be just the thing.

10 p m "Just come back from the pub, the team bonding was not a success as only a couple turned up for a short while and left. The main topic of conversation in the pub was the job of course, various theories were bantered around on one hand, they say to us it's not dangerous job every task will be risk assessed on its merit and if deemed to risky we will no do it, but on the other hand we know it is. They're talking about the possibility of vibrations from the jet propping setting the ballistic missiles off, and the unaccounted torpedo's being in an unstable state. They are talking about things like that, yet at the same time saying it's not dangerous; contradictory to say the least, but we'll persevere."

We haven't had much contact with the Russians but they sound really professional. I've been told they are all officers, all senior personnel, the lowest rank is sergeant major but most of them are officers from admirals to captains and God knows what; they all seem to be top boys and they all seem alright from what I've seen of them so far. They were the divers who were on the first trips to the site with the "Seaway Eagle" and the "Regalia" They retrieved the secret equipment they did not want the west to see and bodies from some of the Compartments. They seem conscientious enough, reading the manuals but the sail out should be interesting because that's where the facade, if any, all comes off. We've got some Dutch divers and obviously a Dutch salvage company so they want to try and get their own Dutch boys on the job. The Dutch divers have only just completed their bloody course; have only been qualified since last Tuesday. And they want them to go out on a job like this. The expertise of the people we have is the best in the world. To send a couple of guys on a course and expect them to be able to perform at this level is unfair to them and their dive partners who need to rely on them and be confident in their ability. We're going to let them go through the motions but I'd be surprised if they actually end up on the job. As a supervisor I'm not going to take people with no experience in "sat" diving on a job as important as this. I don't want to worry about them on diving side as well as the important side of the work. I need to be confident in their ability: that they have not dressed properly and that their gas and hot water supply is OK. If they end up on the job, it'll be purely diplomatic, I would have thought. It is also important to see how the Russian divers turn out. I hope they turn out alright because I think it's important that we do use the Russian Federation divers since they are recovering their dead. It's also up to us to protect their divers from being over enthusiastic and to stop them if they in a position that we consider unsafe. Being naval divers they may be prepared to take a higher degree of risk than we would, especially where ordnance is involved. We intend to permit the Russian divers to perform only tasks that we would let a British diver perform. We do not intend to put them in a situation where they might harm themselves, even if it is for their own country.

Another day of risk assessments, I feel we've got the best superintendents , Sean Pople and Wally Wallace on this job they will ask the right questions and demand answers or we will not proceed with what ever task we are asked to perform, safety is paramount for them. I think knowing they are my immediate line management provides me with confidence that they will protect me from any pressure from commercial interests , or country interests for that matter, I believe they won't let that pressure come down to me or any of the other supervisors. At the end of the day we've got a very conscientious team and I think we're all professionals so it should go all right.

5ᵗʰ July

Just finished the risk assessments, A bit like yesterday, a lot of unknowns, tasks they don't know how they are going to do, what are the plans and the way we are going to do it. Consequently, the safety side of it we can't risk assess because we don't know what it will involve. There is still the issue of ordnance. What's there, and how we are to deal with it. We still believe there are some secrecy issues that they are not telling us. The nuclear boys were giving their side of the risk assessment and I heard indirectly that the reactors on their subs are not stable on a lift; If there's any kind of tilt during the lift these rods which have been retracted from the reactors therefore making them safe could slide back into the reactor itself and re- arm it,, so that's another scary issue. We are really struggling in the dark a bit here about what we are actually going to do on the safety side of it. We're doing everything we can to minimise these risks. We have some of the best people to do that but we need the information and that's not forthcoming from the Russians. Our questions are inevitably answered with "it will be referred to the Russian Federation for consultation." Maybe once we're a bit more isolated at sea they may be a bit more forthcoming but at the end of the day we're not going to do anything we're not happy with. We'll stop until our questions are answered to our "satisfaction before we proceed.

Later that same day "We've were told that we are sailing tomorrow night. We've also been told we've all got to take medicals and blood tests so that we know what our radiation level is before we leave, If anything crops up on this job, sickness or whatever, then they'll have a level of what we had before we left. We all have to visit the doctor onboard for blood samples to be taken we are also still waiting for bits of equipment to arrive. We have been given a sail time of letting the ropes go at 16oohrs tomorrow that will be cutting it fine to get the remaining equipment here in time.

Some of the issues risen to date could put back the sail time. The sail's supposed to be tomorrow but I've got a feeling that they might hold back for maybe a day. We still have the sail over, which is five days, for them to provide answers to our questions. We will also have some time in port in Norway while we do our diving trials and backloads the equipment that will be stored ashore in Norway until required.

Once we sail it'll be less hectic. It's always better once you get going. When we're happy with the sea trials and happy everything else is working fine we will mobilise the rest of the team, our divers and the rest of our topside personnel, once they are onboard we will be ready to sail for the work site. Tonight could be our last run ashore we hope we can entice the Russians out so we can have a few beers together and make some new friends.

The divers by this time knew the broad outline of the situation. As reported on BBC Online the following day the operation would consist of three main stages –
1. Preparing the holes in the hull of the sub for lifting, cutting of the front section
2. Fastening cables to the hull
3. Raising the hull

What they did not know and what was not made clear, was the amount and type of ordnance still aboard the "Kursk" and what were the possible risks of moving the vessel were

Meanwhile on the 6th JULY we felt we needed to get to know our new Russian colleagues better, *We were out last night , had a few beers . We were hoping the Russians would come out but they didn't seem to be that keen on coming. Whether it's just the price of things or were not allowed to we don't know. We've been loading stores all day; the back deck is now getting pretty full. Once we've got on all the big equipment we require for the job onboard, they are going to fill up all the little gaps in-between with gas quads (64 bottle packs of O2 and helium), and cutting oxygen to take along with us to store in Norway.*

We had nuclear radiation induction today, an hour long lecture which really put the wind up us. They were trying to reassure us really. They ended it by saying that the only problem would be if we cut into the hull and there was a gas bubble which would engulf the vessel. Then we all die. Thank you very much.

The lecture I referred to was given by ABC Opleidin they laid out in a flip chart form the basic hazards of Alpha, Beta and Gamma radiation. Alpha radiation, they were told, is only hazardous in the event of internal radiation by ingestion or penetration of wounds. Beta radiation, by contrast, can penetrate the skin and cause burns, but even it can be prevented by a barrier as flimsy as a few millimetres of low density metal or plastic. Gamma radiation, however, is of a different order. Shielding needed against it involves lead or concrete barriers.

If the reactors of the "Kursk" were compromised, Depending on the level of exposure the divers could expect the following effects:-

0-.25 Sv dose - no obvious injury

0.25 - 0.50 Sv dose - possible blood changes

0.50 - 1.00 Sv dose - blood cell changes, some injury, but no disability

1.00 - 2.00Sv dose - possible injuries, disability, nausea and vomiting within 24 hours

2.00 - 4.00 Sv dose - injury and disability certain, death possible

>4.00 Sv dose - 50% probability of death

A one Servits high radiation dose to the whole body gives 80 fatal cancers in a population of a thousand.

The lecture dealt with the precautions necessary when the divers near contaminated sites and the remedies they would need in case clothing or gloves or masks got contaminated. They were told how to use dosimeters, an instrument about the size of a small transistor radio, when they were on station, as well as the use of alarm dosimeters with digital display, which was the size of a large match box.

Well that's it if we have forgotten anything now it's too late we are on our way to Norway. The camera crews are fading into the distance and we can now get on with the task in hand

7th JULY

Quarter past eight in the morning - over the past `12 hours we've been giving instruction to the divers, getting the boat ready, a bit of preparation work for the job ahead. The Russians did show us a picture of the sister ship taken from a video which they brought as a reference for them when marking out the submarine out they permitted us to see there top secret submarine that is base at Murmansk. They indicated to us where they were going to make the holes. In between the bulkheads, the outer hull and the inner hull, there seemed to be a mass of pipe work, ballast tanks, etc. It's not going to be easy. . Also I discovered that Russian divers have been on the submarine and recovered bodies from all the different Compartments and checked the radiation on them. (Apparently they can check from the dentine on the teeth) and this confirmed there was no radiation leak down there. It was the real reason why the bodies were recovered from different compartments in the first place.

8th JULY

Seven o'clock in the morning. Just finished my shift been to the gym and I'm knackered.

We've been training the divers through the night. The Russians are quite keen to learn, I'll give them that. It is a big plus as far as we are concerned that they are willing to take instruction from us. We were talking about the methods we're going to use to uncover the torpedoes which is the jet prop blasting it away. They are very concerned about that, or appeared to be. But as they were talking in Russian I couldn't understand a word they were saying. They were adamant that they need to know how much down thrust there will be in the torpedo area, which doesn't bear thinking about, considering that most of these guys have actually been into the submarine. So they must know a lot more than they are letting on to us. I did ask if they had any more of the submarine video and they said yes but it's not on board. Still holding back information.

9th JULY

It's ten to seven in the morning. Just finished my shift and we've been training the Russians again through the night. They seem to be picking it up alright and don't seem to be having many problems.. We're doing quite well considering the language barrier.

There was a rumour on the Internet that said that the Russians were going to refurbish this submarine, try and re-use it. I put that to one of the Russians through the interpreter and he just laughed and said they were going to cut it up it will be in no condition to re-use.

This refers to the statement, on the "Kursk" website (Kursk. strana.ru) made by Academician Igor Spassky, the head of the Rubin design bureau in St. Petersburg that when raised the submarine would be "utilised" next year (2002)

In dive control there are some old books. The interpreter, Alexei, picked up the novel "Red Storm rising" which is all about when Russia invades Europe by just marching straight through. I was explaining to them what it was about and they seemed to think it was quite amusing. I told them that our governments keep us in a situation of fear for each other so that they can continue building up their military might.

I've got to sign a bit of paper tomorrow saying that I'm not going to discuss this job with anyone outside the need to know circle, or try to steal bits of the submarine or take unofficial photos, this is a top secret job!!t. I am a bit concerned about signing something like that in case it has other implications. I don't mean bits of submarine, I don't give a shit about that, it's more that if something happens and they try to use that to stop us talking - if it's a safety thing - something like a leak, and we are not allowed to report it. They said it's nothing to do with that. We'll see. I'll give it a good read and see if it is trying to restrict my freedom of speech.

10th JULY

Last night we did a bit more training and familiarisation with the Russian divers and we're starting to get on quite well with them. They are obviously good lads and they showed us some of the video they'd taken when leaving St. Petersburg, going to Aberdeen, to getting on the boat. They must have been followed by cameras all the way.

I found out on the internet last night they are saying the missiles on this submarine are the most advanced ever and that no other country has developed any means of tracking them, they are intimating most of the developed nations in the world would love to get their hands on them for there technology. They are called ship wreckers, apparently, and even without a charge they can hit a ship and still sink her. They were also saying that the vibration from the wire ropes when we're cutting the front section off could easy set one off. It's all up to the ordnance specialists when they arrive onboard to tell us what we can or can't do if we come across any of this ordnance. We're right up now on the edge of the artic circle coming round the tip of Norway its so beautiful up here everything seems fresh and clean, Norway is a beautiful country I have been promising myself to bring my wife here for a visit for years.

11th JULY

Our intention is to put the Russian divers in the water to-day or tomorrow for some wet trials we will lower the divers in the diving bells just below the vessel about eight meters. We'll do that all day and tomorrow, that will give us a chance to look at the Russian divers to see how they manage with our equipment. It will also give us a chance to work with the Russian supervisors working through the interpreter we have a chance to work out any problems that may arise, before we get to Kirkenes on Friday.

We were shown a folder which has a lot of photographs which the Russians have waited purposely till we had left UK to hand out to us. They are of the "Kursk" on the seabed as she is now, taken on the previous missions. There were a couple of photos of the inside of the torpedo housing, which is what we are worried about. A picture of the silos showed the missiles, these secret ones that nobody can track. Who would have thought a year ago that I'd have such a document in my hands? What would our American brethren give for that?

We had a demonstration of the cutting machine today; I'll reserve judgement until I see it working but it doesn't look that simple. I've seen one work before and I was impressed with it then. The big difference this time it's the anti-sonar rubber, a good section of it is honeycombed. I think this will cause problems for the cutter ,the operators seem confident though, they assure us that a specimen of the rubber was given to them for trials and they insist there won't be a problem !!. Ill reserve judgement then.

12th JULY

There have been murmurings among the troops about wanting a bonus or danger money. I think they're trying to make a case for a bonus, partly because a lot of things are coming to light now we have arrived. Personally I came out knowing what the money was, it's a bit late to ask for more money. The important thing is the insurances we've have in place, we can stop at any time and pull off in we consider it to dangerous. So long as this condition is unquestionable then it's not a problem really. As far as I'm concerned, having the responsibility of a supervisor, if I come across something I consider to dangerous or unsafe we will stop and reassess our position. I have the authority to stop the job, and in conjunction with the OPMs(offshore project managers Wally Wallace & Sean Pople) we can decide to recover everybody, pull off, and re-think our position. I think our company will back any decision we may come to. Sean & Wally (OPM) will back us all the way and are articulate and diplomatic enough to convince the Dutch and Russians that it's the best course of action. With that in mind I do not foresee any problems we won't be able to overcome.

According to some of the lads who phoned home last night, the BBC news reported that the British Government are trying to stop the job. As I understand it, they are under pressure from Norway who is concerned about contamination.   I think it's a bit of sensationalism by the media they have to dramatise as much as they can for their stories.

Today is the first time we've put the Russians in the water, only down to about three meters, just to get a look at them and get them to look at our equipment. They seemed to do all right – no problem. They are sticklers for paper work, who's got to go in with whom. It is all stipulated which Russian diver will go in the water with which partner, unlike us anybody can dive with anyone, it must be written down, and the Admiral's got to approve it.   This makes the paperwork a bit over the top but its there system and we have to adapt, after all technically they are our clients. Just like any clients in the North Sea we work to their system.

I was in the gym with the Admiral himself (Gennady Verrich) and his second in command was with him. He's quite amicable really for an Admiral, always smiling and says hello he looks quite fit too. We tried to converse a little but it's hard if you do not speak Russian and he has no English.

I am starting to get a bit of rap ore going now with some of the Russians - a couple of them have quite a bit of character It's good to see; bearing in mind the sort of doctrine we have been fed - about them coming over, slaughtering us and eating our babies; the usual shit. They are ordinary people like us; I would like to know what they have been told about us.

13th JULY

It's Friday the 13th I hope not a bad omen!!! We are just outside Kirkenes now ready to go in – pilot's on board. Apparently the world press are waiting for us.

I gave some lectures yesterday to the Russian team on emergencies and drills, both what we need to do and what we expect from them. We did some testing on the bell - had a bit of a problem with communications but that's all sorted. We did a test dive just to check that everything was working fine.

Another day of diving tomorrow, the rest of the dive team should be joining us onboard and we have some training with the ordnance people. They are going to give us a lecture and some more training on the nuclear aspect of the job.

The Russians had a big meeting last night to see who is staying on and who is going off, as there is something like eight or ten divers and only four are staying. We presume the others will come out and relieve them at a later date. I walked in on the meeting inadvertently and they all stared at me because it's not the done thing to interrupt the Admiral during a briefing.

Kirkenes is so far north that at this time of the year they do not have any night, there is no setting sun. It's been day all the time. It's the weirdest feeling if you've never had it before. Outside working at 12 0 clock midnight and its still broad daylight is a weird feeling.

The old doctor, Sergei, was at my lecture yesterday and he was interested in how we treat the guys in "sat" if there's an injury. He kept throwing this scenario up at me - what if the divers can't do this, what if the divers can't do that. I mean, we're all trained in first aide and some of us are very advanced, so dealing with serious injuries is not uncommon for us. He was just building this scenario up and up, I eventually told him the patient will die if the scenario is that bad, this stunned him for a minute. I did add that it's a very rare occasion when a fatality occurs. I just said we'd manage most situations. He did say there would be a hospital ship in the vicinity which is going to have surgeons and doctors at our disposal, so that's good to know.

I have heard today that the Danes are supposed to be trying to stop us as well. Now we've got the Danes, Norwegians, and the UK all trying to stop starting this mission. We'll persevere until they drag us off.

On a more serious note: under the surface of all the joviality on board, we do know it's a graveyard as well. There are over a hundred people still in that submarine down there; I think the way we deal with it is by making light of everything else and not mentioning the loss of life but I think it's not to far from everyone's thoughts. I think we are also aware that we will come across these bodies. Our policy is treating them with dignity and respect. The Russian divers are supposed to deal with any body issues but if they are not available we have body bags onboard and I am sure the lads are capable of dealing with the problem if it arises. There are going to be situations like that which are serious, I know. Its there in the back of your mind but if you dwell on it to much it will stress you out.

As we surveyed the quayside at this most northerly part of Norway it is the last large settlement before you enter into Russia we am concerned about waiting newsmen, we are still wary of getting bad press which could jeopardise the job. There are people alongside the jetty, and the news media of the world waiting. I've got a feeling the Captain is not going to permit the divers going ashore, I am sure the last thing they want on this media sensitive project is for a diver to go ashore get a few beers inside him and start shooting his mouth of to the world press. With a few beers inside him he will probably say what ever they want him to. So I'd be surprised if they let the crew go ashore.

14TH JULY

Expected to sail today but the rumours are rife about what's going on; nobody seems to know. The rumours vary from there being no insurance on the vessel and we can't sail until we get it; to equipment not turning up for radiation training.

We had a big meeting yesterday, to continue the risk assessments for the bits that weren't resolved in Aberdeen. At the end of the day a lot of it is still not resolved. A lot of the smaller stuff has been resolved, but our main concern has been the ordnance and the ordnance specialist hasn't turned up yet so we are still in the dark on are main concerns. We've only been clearance to ROV (Remotely Operated Vehicle) the worksite when we do get permission to sail. We can also deploy the transponder array for radiation monitoring and we can mark out the Compartments on the outer hull for removal. But that's all we can do - no more intervention than that.

I spoke to Justin, the surveyor last night. He will deploy and calibrate the transponder array. He was saying he is on his own and he still has to put all this information together and do all the calibration. It normally takes a team of lads a couple of days. But he's on his own.

The jet propping is only supposed to take two days. Rumours abound that it's going to take at least one to two weeks. I just think we're all in rumour mongering mode right now. We're all convinced there is something they're not telling us about this bloody submarine. The gist of it is that, deep down; we all believe there are maybe a couple of missiles on there with nuclear warheads, even though the Russian categorically deny this. It seems to me to be the biggest worry to most of the divers who may come across them.

I was speaking to the Russians last night in the video room, having a laugh and a joke. I think they're all generally nice ordinary guys but you get the feeling they are not fully in the picture themselves. They know obviously, what they are doing, but being a military regime they just get told what the authorities want them to know and they don't ask questions. We were to my surprise allowed ashore last night but the Russians were not permitted to leave the vessel. I asked the interpreter "aren't they allowed to go ashore?" He said that the Admiral hadn't said that they couldn't go ashore. So I asked if that meant that he also hadn't said that they could, and he said "that's right". So they don't bother. In some ways this will avoid any embarrassing situations for them as it is very expensive in Norway at £5 a pint of beer it would be very expensive on a Russian sailors pay. Our crew put in an appearance in the town they all seem to end up in the local hotel where they met up with the on coming crew. Under the influence of many Norwegian beers some decided to accompany the guys who were staying in the hotel before joining ship in the morning to their rooms. Where they drank the contents of their mini bars dry before returning to the ship. There will be some sore heads and big bar bills to be paid for in the morning. I was working on deck through the night and had a grandstand view of the lads meandering back to the ship trying to negotiate the gangway totally oblivious to my presence and sometime assistance getting them aboard.

15th JULY

We set sail at 8 o'clock last night, the 14th, with a little bit of a send off at Kirkenes. There were a couple of film crews there, a few people to wave us off. As we went majestically down the fjord there was a little replica Viking boat with full sail and as we went past it set off a little cannon and they all waved to us.

Before we sailed I went down into the town yesterday after shift just for a walk, and thought I would buy some beers for the Russian Navy lads because they've not been allowed to go ashore, it's expensive here so as a gesture of friendship I thought I'd get them a few cans so they could have a little drink before we set sail. I brought them back and went to the skipper and told him what I'd proposed. It was not the response I had hoped for due to the sensitive nature of the job the captain could not condone alcohol onboard. I tried to reason the fact we were about to go to sea and they hadn't been allowed ashore, there would only be about half a can each so they're hardly going to get shit-faced. But no, he was adamant it was a dry ship. He did relent to let us drink them on the jetty. So I spoke to the Admiral through the interpreter. I felt a little embarrassed to say I've brought some beer for your crew but you cannot drink it on the vessel - only on the jetty. He said he would think about it. I felt I had offended him but before I had reached the door he said yes, it's ok. So at six o'clock we met on the jetty and just had these few cans of beer. It was nice just to relax with the Russians. We didn't have enough to let our hair down exactly, but it's just that people are different when you're talking over a beer. I think the Russian lads appreciated it because later on during the night they came and gave me one of the insignias for the Navy Submarine Fleet and a badge for the Northern Fleet, because they're all members. I was quite chuffed!

When we sailed and left the fjord we were immediately tracked by a Russian frigate as our escort out to the Kursk accident site. Apparently there are a couple of ships there guarding it, and have been ever since the accident. We had some more nuclear instructions today and all got issued with our little rad counter badges, which have to stay with us all the time. So we've all got those dangling round our necks.

We got hold of the report from the nuclear advisory people about the situation in general about what has been dumped in various seas around the world; like submarines with nuclear reactors, as obviously this isn't the first. Apparently they used to just dump old nuclear reactors well out at sea there has never been any significant leakage from those. They just explained what has gone on before, what they've done; Obviously the Russians have been inside the Kursk on the previous missions and recovered all their sensitive material from the operations room and also, recovered a few of the bodies.

It was sad to read in this report that they found one of the bodies and it had a letter taped to him to say that they had survived the initial explosion and had moved into the furthest Compartment; but he had not survived   That must have been a horrendous way to go. I suspect hypothermia would have got to them first so at least that's not as bad as being burnt to death or worse. It's a bit morbid. Like I said before, we all realise we're going to a graveyard and I think that will be in the back of all our minds for the duration of the project.

We have one of these radiation monitors for the inside of the diving bells - one of only six in the world apparently brought in to monitor the radiation in the bell for the divers. The radiation specialist told us how great this machine was when I asked him it will work under pressure in a wet environment he said with all the confidence he could muster that it would. Guess what it did not.

A couple of lads woke up to a pleasant surprise, because of a bunk shortage they are to be temporally billeted on the hospital ship. Due to a visit from a Russian delegation their bunks and lifeboat place will be required. It is said that the hospital ship is full of frustrated nurses, vodka and they will be treated like royalty, wishful thinking I think. The Russian divers brought them down to earth; they warned them to take food because it was terrible on there.

16ᵗʰ JULY

We have arrived on the site now - over the "Kursk" We were escorted into the 500 metre zone (this is an exclusion zone around the submarine which the Russian Navy are not permitting any vessels to enter) and we've got three ships around us - what looks like a destroyer, quite a big one, a small frigate; and a small civilian or merchant navy one.   We had some helicopters coming and going all yesterday morning bringing all these top brass. The Admiral of the whole Northern Fleet was on board and he was joined by   the designer of the submarine and a couple more experts. Information should be at our beck and call with so much expertise and power onboard.

On a more sombre note, the Russians held service at eight o'clock yesterday evening because, as I said before, there are a lot of their dead comrades down there. We were all invited we had a minute's silence and a prayers were said by the skipper. All the Russian navy lads were lined up, said a few prayers and threw some flowers into the sea – a very poignant moment. When the service was over a small boat from one of the guard ships came along side to take of the Russian divers who were not to take part in the salvage but were to remain on the guard ship as reserves. It was quite touching to see the way they parted; hugging and holding hands and "see you later" sort of thing. They're a bit more" hands on "than us reserved Brits, a couple of them left. It was quite a significant moment we were about to start the biggest whole salvage ever attempted.

At nine o'clock our ROV went in the water, our small observation rov called the "Tiger".   The bigger one known as the "Work Class" was to remain on standby. The "Tiger" descended to about eighty meters. We then had the radioactive guy running around, doing his scanning the umbilical as we recovered it to the surface. To do the survey we had to deploy the "Work Class". As you can imagine there were a lot of people around the camera monitors trying to get their first glimpse of the submarine. Because they were doing the approach survey and checking for radiation levels it was a very slow progress.   The ROV has been mapping out the area to confirm that the co-ordinates given are the right ones. Then survey can produce the overlays for our TV monitors in dive control. Once that is completed they can then start mapping out the submarine.

The intention is to finish surveying then put in the jet prop which is going to clear the silt and debris away from the forward compartment which is our intention to remove; hopefully this will expose any unexploded ordnance that might be in this area.

We're putting anti restraining wires in the radiation monitoring equipment's umbilicals, to prevent tension on the delicate wires, and we're trying to get the procedures for the decontamination and radioactivity changed. Some guy in Belgium, who's never been on a Dive Support Vessel before, has sat at his desk and wrote out these procedures and his representative onboard insists that we adhere to them to the letter, which is totally impractical. We're trying to get him to change them, but he's one of those "jobsworth" types: got to do it as it's written - if it's got to change then somebody else has to make that decision. We need people onboard prepared to make decisions and adapt the procedures to the job in hand. It's very frustrating for us.

My collection of Russian Naval insignia badges was increased by one to-day it was a badge which represented you as a member of the Russian Dive Team I was very flattered but also a little embarrassed because it had obviously been cut from one of their own uniforms. These badges or any gift are not given openly I was asked to come to one side and it was surreptitiously placed in my hand with a wink and a nod as if to say there you go mate. My collection is growing to the envy of my workmates.

By the 17th the BBC News Online reported that there were eight vessels in the vicinity, including one carrying journalists. Several "underwater objects had been spotted, from the air, trying to approach the "Kursk" one senior Russian official fumed. But he was able to crow that the Russian naval vessels had driven them away. We were unaware of this international drama carrying on around us.

17th JULY

During the last 24 hours the hospital ship has arrived. It looks like a liner or cruise ship a big white beast she is standing of now outside the 500m zone. It's comforting to know that we've got a well equipped hospital standing by with surgeons and an operating theatre onboard. We also found out that the doctor onboard is considered to be their top man in the Russian Navy, Chief Surgeon, we are receiving top billing here.

Yesterday we had access to the submarine for the first time and we managed to have a good look round to get our bearings. It's not quite what the media led us to believe. The silt build up at the front , which we thought would take quite a while to clear using the jet prop, is not as severe as first thought, Inside the front compartment there doesn't seem to be much left that is recognisable. The ROV went inside the nose today and what a mess it looked! There's been some severe explosion here, the ROV managed to get through as far as the conning tower. The ROV pilot who was flying was accompanied by one of the designers of the submarine sat close beside him. He was asking to go here and go there, but when the senior navy admiral, discovered this by watching on the bridge monitor and realising they were inside the front section he went pretty ballistic and shouted "get out of there, get out of there. You shouldn't be in there" It's ridiculous this secrecy thing .We need to know what the state of the Compartment is, before we enter. If they will not let us survey the area we cannot appraise the safety and stability of the Compartment. The Admiral pulled us out of there and only permitted us to survey the debris around the forward Compartment. They continued with the survey that the Admiral permitted us which was around the submarine, we plotted any debris found and seabed samples were taken to check radiation levels. The samples came back as normal and we were permitted to enter the front section to take water samples only, which are being tested as I right this. We don't expect any high

45

readings because the mud samples were clear - the readings were no higher than normal background readings. The Russians Navy and the designers were not happy with each other, Rubens (the designers) were not to happy to have been over ruled by the Navy. They now apparently have got to talk to some guy in St Petersburg before giving us the ok to proceed. We are standing by now. .

We watched the jet prop promotional video to see the techniques we're going to using while we are waiting for the thumbs up to start. Smit also said they may get the jet prop people to jet prop where the suction anchor are intended to be positioned. These suction anchors will be used to mount the pulley wheels for the cutting wire that will be used to remove the front section they need to be at least one metre below the outer hull of the submarine to ensure the cut will pass al the way through. The suction anchors are huge cylinders about 6 metres in diameter and 30 metres long. On top they have a hose connection which can pressurise or suck out the air inside causing a vacuum this then enables the anchor to bury itself into the seabed or to extract itself depending on which function you need it to perform at the time. It's amazing how easily it works. The holes that the jet prop make will make it easier for the anchors to achieve the seal at the base of the anchor to seabed, which is required for it to work. ..

Once they finish the jet prop work we will return to Kirkenes drop off all this jet prop manpower and equipment then we can mobilise the cutting equipment and men. There will be a certain amount of deck chess to get their equipment in place. Then we can return to the site and start getting stuck in to the job, that's what everybody is itching to do now.

We spent some time today translating our names into Russian and putting them on our hats for the Russians. Old Shep, our resident interpreter has been doing a good job. He's only got one wrong so far. It's quite amusing to see the Russians reading your hat and saying "ah - Reynaldo or ah Dave"

I was talking to Andreas today one of the Russian divers, a good lad. He wants to get going, all the training he has been doing for this job he wants to get started, and everyone has that edge about them now the sooner we get started the better.

18th JULY

We had a risk assessment done on the vessel and they concluded that this vessel, the "Mayo" can withstand two sub sea torpedo explosions with little damage - maybe a good shake of the vessel - a few seals would possibly fail - a few things would fall off the bulkheads, but that's about it. When we start jet propping we were just told we had to have the minimum number of people below the water line they believe that if there is to be an explosion it could be during this phase. The prop has been going for a couple of hours not without to much success they have got down 0.5 to 0.8 of a metre which has removed the soft silt and now have hit clay. The intention is to recover the prop and install the clay cutter. This consists of sections of chain hanging down from the bottom of the prop, the prop is lowered closer to the seabed and the jet propulsion is enough to agitate the chain to hopefully churn up the clay so it can be blown away, it's a painfully slow process but it needs to be done to uncover any rogue torpedoes.

I walked in on the Russian divers in the recreation room last night and they all had their heads round a load of photographs. I said before about this bloody secrecy thing, we're all on the same side here with the same aims.. They were actually looking at the torpedoes. I managed to get a look over their shoulders but they sort of manoeuvred me away. One of the supervisors showed me a little picture but it was only a torpedo. They seem to think we've got our own agenda here, to get as many secrets as *we can. I'm sure they have this vision of me selling state secrets to the USA which of course is nonsense. (Unless the money is right)*

On the internet yesterday it said we were doing the most dangerous job in the world, what heroes we all are. Which just makes us laugh a little, especially in one of the dailies it's apparently reporting we are getting £2000 per man per day. Wish that were true. I'll actually end up getting less than I normally do on a job in the UK because of tax I'm actually worse off. Don't know where they got that one from, especially with our personnel manager, saying it's not a dangerous job you can't have extra money. We need to cut out all these comments from the papers and send them to him.

19th JULY

To-day I have woken to find we are sailing back to Kirkenes. They've finished the jet propping. They've cleared along the cut area down to a meter below the bottom of the submarine. The Smit Tech salvage master was happy with that. The Russians weren't. They wanted more but it's a commercial decision they will argue it out with the Russians.

The ATM Carrier (the cutting barge) ,is a flat top barge which is now in Holland, its going to be towed up here , which will take about ten days. Then it will have a couple of days in Kirkenes for more work to be done on her before she comes out to us. It'll be a couple of weeks before she gets onto the job site. We'll just continue cutting holes in the submarine until it arrives. . Then we'll pull off and let her take up station over the submarine. We will give it any assistance it needs, and let it cut the front Compartment off. Once that has been accomplished she can bugger off and we can get back to work cutting the holes. When we have completed preparing the holes we will be ready for the Giant 4 Lift barge. She will lift the Kursk and transport it to Murmansk to dry dock it's quite straight forward really!!!.

Had a chance to chat last night with the Russian Admiral through the interpreter. We just started chatting about things in general, he was in charge when they first came up to do the initial rescue with the "Seaway Eagle". He openly said they didn't let the British divers do too much, just let them look around the outside, because there was obviously lots of stuff to take out, which is understandable - secrets and all that. I asked if the Russian dive team were going ashore. He said "oh no can't go ashore". It also looks like they are going to be here for the full duration of the job how ever long that might be.

20th JULY

We are In Kirkenes now we have worked hard through the night to get the jet prop equipment off and the NCA (Norwegian Cutting & Abandonment) grit cutting equipment onboard, loads of welding, taking off gear, putting on gear. All the Russians managed to get ashore and enjoyed themselves. The Admiral must have given them a reprieve. But they always go en masse, all together and come back together. It was nice when they asked if I'd go with them, but at the time I was unloading a truck, so I was up to my eyes in it and wasn't able to go. I think they just had a look round the town, which has a most interesting history. It was the most bombed place during the whole of the Second World War. It was constantly fought over between the Russians and the Germans. Whoever controlled Kirkenes could destroy or protect the Atlantic convoys which sailed in and out of Murmansk.

The first British team went into "sat" at 11 o'clock last night. It was going to be a Russian team (two Russians and a Brit) but because the Russians wanted a bit more training and familiarisation with the cutting gear we put a Brit team in.

I was speaking to the NCA guys today. These Norwegians will be in charge of the cutting gear. They were the ones who went over and did the tests in Murmansk at the submarine base. They think the cutter worked quite well. We have reservations. There are 8 cms. Of solid rubber and 2 cms of honeycomb rubber before you reach the 10cms. of steel plate. They claim their cutting equipment can cut through the whole lot in one pass. I believe that the honeycomb rubber will disperse the high pressure cutting jet, preventing it from cutting through the steel plate. On most systems, if you get an air gap between the jet and plate being cut then it will not work properly. But NCA are claiming that they have overcome this problem. It'll be interesting to see. .

Some bright spark worked out there's 300 meters of cutting to do at so many centimetres per hour, which worked out at about 290 hours of cutting. That doesn't include all the setting up and moving around. So it's a lot of cutting and time. When I was speaking to the admiral the other night I mentioned this statistic to him and he said he would be surprised if we were ready to pick the submarine up in time. My feeling is that if we pick the "Kursk" up this year, we'll be very lucky. Everything has got to go just right - no weather problems.

We're sailing out from Kirkenes now into bad weather - not bad enough for us not to dive but if it picks up any more it will be a problem. When we go out this time I don't suppose we'll be coming back for a while. We've got all the equipment we require now and they're going to re-supply us at sea. The ATM Carrie (the cutting barge) has set sail now. The estimated time of arrival is about two weeks. It has some equipment that we will need but we'll just have to wait for it.

21ˢᵗ JULY

Well' we did our first dive last night at one o'clock, with the Russians. Let's put it this way - it was a steep learning curve for them. They seemed to be a bit apprehensive, which is understandable. There's should be nothing new here. They've been thrown in at the deep end, so to speak. They seem to have a pathological fear of the ROV that it is going to kill them, which it isn't they continued with the marking out the holes on the outer hull with special templates they brought with them from Russia. One of the divers was very cold in the neck area. It must be a suit problem or something, he came back early.

It's very hard to supervise a dive with a Russian supervisor and an interpreter and the Admiral to boot! Also in attendance were the other supervisor, the doctor, every man and his dog telling us what to do? It's got to be sorted out. There are too many people in dive control trying to give us orders. We've got the Brit team going in next. Just the fact that they are experienced people means they should get a lot done. The first dive for the Russians was OK we have to be more productive though if we have any hope of getting the sub up this year.

We had the radiation man blowing a fuse because he says he needs to check all the wires and umbilical with his hand held device as we recover the bell which is not practical it would take a couple of hours to recover the bell using his method. If he insists on this he will be working 24/7 and I can't see that happening. We have named him ""Peter, the spy" because of his close association with the Smit Tak salvage master. His insistence on knowing everything is going on he is in and out of dive control all the time. Any information he gleams he relays back to the salvage master, but because of his height *he keeps banging his head on the door every time he comes in to dive control, poor sod. Still you've got to have someone to take the piss out of on shift.*

22nd JULY

When I went on shift last night, they'd got the cutting gear down which is designed to cut through the echo absorber, which is two or three inches of thick dense rubber then a honeycombed layer of after that and if that's not enough, there's 10mm of steel hull. Once it was all set up for the first cut we had lots of problems with hydraulics. We had to stand by for a few hours until their technicians repaired them .When they eventually did attempt our first cut, the machine worked for a few minutes then the hydraulics failed again. We made the machine safe went to inspect our efforts, to our frustration this very expensive cutting machine on which the majority of the cutting phase depends on had only managed to penetrate a couple of inches of the rubber a roaring success it was not. Hopefully we should be starting again shortly. The NCA guys (cutting machine specialists) have been up for something like forty hours, and they needed sleep so we put them to bed. With luck after some sleep they should be up for trying another cut, fingers crossed with better results, we got a lot riding on this cutter.

We can still make some progress with the Russian divers, the measuring & marking of the outer hull sections to be removed with the cutter still has to be done. There could be a problem; if we complete the marking out and the cutter is not working all work will come to a standstill until its working properly.

A few hours have passed and the Russian divers are marking out compartment VI this is where the nuclear reactors are. We have instigated a no lift area over section VI any crane work on the vessel is forbidden just in case the unlikely happens and we drop a load from the vessel the impact damage to the reactor area could be catastrophic. This exclusion zone will also apply to the silo areas as.

I have been designated a Russian team to supervise for the foreseeable future, it is very time consuming and frustrating having every word I say is translated to Russian then re-laid to the Russian Supervisor, if he has any questions that has to be translated to me, my answers are then translated again for the supervisor, and then invariably the Admiral has to be consulted his questions answered and with any luck this will be passed on to the diver. To make matters worse everything has to be written down on what we call a dive plan, this document outlines the work scope for that particular dive, I have a plan and the Russians have a translated version the problem arises when you ask the diver to perform a task which has not been written on the dive plan no matter how mundane that task is i.e. if I asked for the diver to take a particular tool with him for a task the Russian supervisor would be argue, that it is not on the dive plan so he will not take it with him. This then would end in a big debate about why or why not this tool should be taken, the Admiral would be informed and a decision made. This is happening all the time and no work is being performed, with our short timescale we can not afford to waste this much time. I do have some empathy for Russians they are not commercial divers and are not used to the same work methods we employ for our divers; time is money in the commercial game. Unless they up the work rate 200% the Smit Tak guys will want them out of sat and Brits or Dutch in. This is still early days we haven't even started cutting yet and some clever clog's has worked out that there is 300mtrs of cutting to go.

I am trying to get a bit of humour going with the Russians break down a few barriers they are very stand offish .We had a visit from one of their senior representatives to-day he was wearing a pair of coveralls which were green and yellow an exact copy of a BP forecourt attendant. When he left and I explained this through the interpreter to the Russians in dive control there was an uneasy silence at first then they all saw the funny side. From that point on every time he came in we asked for 50 litres of unleaded. I felt this was a small step towards gaining their trust.

23rd JULY

When I came on shift tonight the cutting gear hadn't been a successful . They'd had to perform some trials on scrap steel and things like that. Apparently they had started cutting through the rubber but the tracking wasn't working, so we had to recover the machine again for repairs. It's still not working properly now.

The first dangerous task was given to my team to-day; we were assigned the task of going into the forward compartment and look for the unaccounted and unexploded missing torpedoes. My team consisted of Andrea (he was a very big man but a gentle giant he was an officer) Vladimir (he was a nice man very courageous he was not an officer) Alexia was there supervisor he was everything you would expect a Russian officer to be stern, abrupt, disciplinarian. Last but not least was Phil he was the British person on the team designated bellman he was there to look after them in saturation and to operate the complicated equipment. At this time no one had ventured this far forward of the submarine we were not sure what to expect. When both divers were on the top of the submarine they gingerly ventured forward, even though these divers were trained in ordinance work and I myself have worked with explosives in Northern Ireland it was still a tense time. When they reached the beginning of the devastation of the front compartment we looked into a deep black expanse of nothing. Both divers carry hat cameras which relay the pictures back to dive control so we can see what they can see. There was just blackness most people think a diver at 100 metres depth can not see anything but you would be surprised what you can see also the divers have hat lights, but looking into this hole was very eerie. Andrei started to set up a rope to lower himself into the blackness and to god knows what below.

When it was set up and ready for descending Andre turned to Serge and told him to go down all this was going on in Russian but even in a language I did not understand I just knew what had happened being ex military Vladimir was not as senior as Andre so he had to go in first. It is the same the world over!!. When Vladimir lowered himself over the side we were all very tense in dive control wondering what he might be faced with down there. It was a drop of about 9 or 10 metres into the hole and what we found there was complete devastation a mass of steel 2inch thick bent and twisted as if it was plastic .Nothing could be identified we had a couple of design engineers along side us trying to make sense of mess trying to recognise bits of structure with limited success. We had little luck with the structure even less with trying to identify torpedoes, the decision was made to exit this area, return to marking out the outer hull and return here at a later date with a more comprehensive plan. After leaving the front compartment with the divers the overriding feeling was of sorrow for the poor submariners who were in there when the explosion occurred it must have been like a volcano blowing.

The relief dive team arrived as we were continuing with the marking up, according to there dive plan they were going to carry on with the cutting. We needed to retest the cutting gear they've been working on for hours fingers crossed it will work now. However, the Russians had other plans. They weren't going to do the cutting and no matter what we said they were not about to change their plans. Their intention was to carry out marking up the outer hull. We were well advanced in the marking up of the hull, it is imperative that we start cutting it's the most urgent task at this time. Alexia insisted that we adhered to the dive plan he had been given. This is what I was trying to do because the running of the dive was my responsibility, I was insisting we went with the dive plan, well the one I had in my hand. Alex the interpreter solved the dilemma when he read both dive plans he informed me they was totally different plans. It transpired the agreed dive plan (the one I had) was not acceptable to the Russians and they just wrote there own. The Admiral was informed he came into dive control, plenty of raised voices the outcome was use the Russian plan. I believe they were not confident to operate the cutting equipment so reverted to marking up which was more familiar to them. Even though the cutting was very important to get started the Russians prevailed and marking we did, which meant at least another six hours before we could have a Brit team in the water and get the cutter up and working, more lost time. I later found out the last time we visited Kirkenes to offload the Jet Prop equipment, the port visit was not authorised by the Russians and they were very pissed of about it. They were under the impression that once we were on site we going to be there until the submarine was raised. The offloading of equipment and the loading of more because of the deck space was not explained to them properly, so there has been a bit of posturing from the Smit hierarchy and the Russians we are in the middle. The fall out of this is the co-operation from one another is not as good as it could be. To try and relieve the tension they seem to be letting the Russians have their own way a little hence the back down on the dive plan situation. It's a no-win thing at the end of the day and as far as I'm concerned we just want a plan that we can work to and achieve a descent amount of work.

After about three hours into one diver appeared to be overheating himself, a diving suit is a loose fitting neoprene layer it has a network of rubber tubes around full of perforations this carries a flow of hot water around the body which the temperature can be regulated from the surface, so the diver can work in comfort. The suit also has a bypass at the point it enters the suit so the water can be dumped if required i.e. water to hot or the diver wants to cool down a little this will give him some control of his temperature.

This problem happened on the previous dive to the same diver I tried to explain to the Alexia the Russian supervisor about how we can regulate the hot water top side if he is too hot, and how he could dump the water from his suit if need be for what ever reason i.e. the water is too hot or he may need to cool down a little after some exertion. I do not believe this was passed on to the diver, he was becoming more agitated I could hear it in his voice. I am also aware that some divers and I include myself in this have a problem with hot water when breathing helium. The part of the brain that tells you if you are to hot or to cold can be effected when breathing helium your brain tells you are cold but in reality you are hot so you keep asking for the temperature to be raised, normally this is kept in check with the help of the other diver if you ask him if he is OK if he says yes you can be pretty confident the other is too. I was thinking in this case he is getting over heated I did try to intervene but the language was a problem. I did tell the bellman Phil what I thought was happening and to be prepared for an emergency. At that same moment Alexia told me that the diver will be returning to the bell as he was feeling unwell. When we eventually got him back to the bell once his hat was removed he drank a whole litre of water in one go and he was weak as a kitten. This could have been a serious incident it is very easy for things like exhaustion and unconsciousness to occur working in this environment. If a diver becomes unconscious it then becomes our problem to get him back safe. I tried very hard to convey to the Russians how dangerous this was I believe it was some kind of bravado thing with them and considered it a loss of face that this diver had to return to the bell early. After the dive the senior Russian navel officers went down to the chambers and spoke to him they did not seem to show to much concern it sounded like he was getting a roasting. The dive was not to productive what with the problem with the diver and he'd returned to the bell early it left just the one diver to try and mark up by himself which was really a two man job. I did make the suggestion we try and set up the cutting equipment but that was not received to well, at that point the Russian doctor ordered the divers back to bell and terminated the dive. I have never heard of this before a doctor terminating activities it is always the supervisor. I am not sure what is going on here, in the commercial industry you can not afford to recover divers with no team ready to replace them it means a couple of hours standing by while next team woken fed and briefed. I was ready to carry on with the one diver after checking with the bellman, Phil told me the second diver was well and comfortable in the bell there was no emergency as far as I was concerned.

The weather has started to pick up. We're being chucked about a bit now. We have been lucky with the weather up to now, it was bound to come. I hope it does not get too bad we can not afford to loose time to the weather if we are going to pick the sub up this year..

There is a lot of speculation from the media that we will be leaving unexploded torpedoes on the seabed, creating problems for the future that is not the case. The fact is that the forward Compartment which will be cut off is going to be recovered at a future date; it contains valuable evidence of what actually happened on that day.

We have a bit more of a laugh and a joke with the Russians now. Every day we get on a little better. I told them my one and only Russian joke today. A member of the Politburo was visiting an outlying farming region and he stops and talks to a peasant farmer. He says to the farmer" I want you to supply the whole of Moscow with potatoes and cabbages so they can be well fed". The farmer says "But we have cabbages and potatoes piled up so high they are touching the clouds in the sky, we can feed the whole of Mother Russia." The Politburo member says "are you joking with me peasant" The farmer says "Well' you started it." To my amazement they started to laugh.

24th JULY

We've been playing with this NCA cutting gear and it's not working again, this is causing us one big headache. It was reported on the Internet last night that our grit cutting is going very well. We've been at it for two days now and we haven't done one cut yet! One of the guys was talking to his wife who asked when he'd be home. He said "How old is our granddaughter now? She replied" She's only a couple of months." He said "Well, the rate this cutting is going I'll see her when she's about five". That gives some indication of how "well" it's going.

I'm becoming somewhat frustrated because working with the Russians is a bit of a nightmare. They're nice enough people and I have a bit of a laugh with them but try to get them to do anything! They have no sense of urgency, no concept of changing the dive plan half way through, if circumstance change. In this game you have to adapt to what's going on and they don't know how to do that. If it's not on the dive plan they aren't going to do it. They wouldn't use the water jet last night(this a handheld water jet with pressures up to 15000psi used for cleaning or in this case try and cut the anti sonar rubber). They say it's too dangerous and they haven't had enough training on it. This is all bollocks because we have given training to all of them, and continually kept asking them if there was anything else they wanted to go through, anything else at all; but oh no we can master your equipment we are very happy was the reply, no problems. Then first time we ask to deploy the water jet, they're not happy with that and complain how we haven't trained them enough, it's very, very frustrating. The amount of work I got out of them in six hours today I could have done easily in a couple of hours with a Brit diver. No problem at all to us, as a company we are day rate, but for Smit this project is a fixed price, it can cost them dearly. If we are going to keep the Russian dive teams in all through this project it's going to cost them a lot of time and money, because frankly they're not up to it.

Anyway as I finished my shift the next team were just starting another attempt at cutting a hole, more tests and trials, bearing in mind that they'd supposedly done all their tests and trials on the same materials we have encountered here in Murmansk. I don't know what they were testing on but it doesn't seem to be the same material as we have on this submarine.

I mentioned earlier that two Russian divers were sent over to the naval destroyer to be held in reserve. They were recalled today because the Russians decided to pull out the diver, Vladimir because of the problems he was having with over heating. The Russian doctor decided to decompress him. One of the standbys will take his place on the team and the other will accompany him during decompression, which will take about four days. Sergei who replaces Vladimir in the team, was blown(compressed) straight into "sat" and had to dive immediately. It was a shock to the system for him, thrown in the deep so to speak not much time to prepare yourself, but he coped well; no worse than any of the others. I did get the feeling that it was considered a disgrace for poor Vladimir because he was pulled from sat. I think he was considered one of their most experienced and senior divers.

I spoke to the Russians yesterday about a report in the media that the Russian Navy has been chasing off foreign vessels that are trying to get near the "Kursk" site. Apparently a foreign submarine tried to get close, trying to obtain any technical information it could gather, but it was discovered and chased off by the Russian guard vessels. According to the Russians it's not true, they did think it was funny, but they did not confirm or deny the rumour. We told them we thought it might be a Japanese tourist sub.

25ᵗʰ JULY

We started to cut the mast off with a hydraulic saw yesterday(they have to be removed because of the clearance when the submarine is lifted up under the Giant 4 for transportation to Murmansk), but it wasn't working very well. It lasted about four or five hours and we'd only got through about half an inch. We have continued played around with that; we have re-rigged it, changed the hydraulics, and started again. It started to work, so, as I left shift about an hour ago, there was only about an inch left to cut so I expect it will be off by now. Hopefully that's the first of three masts and one sail to be removed the forward mast has a dome on the top this apparently contains all their secret communications and sonar technology. The Naval people onboard seem to think we are doing our utmost to get a look at this dome! the dome is bolted on so the plan is to take it off prepare it for recovery bring a Russian tug along side, bring to surface then transfer to the tug with as little delay as possible this will keep all their secrets safe (as if we give a shit). The funny thing is Rubens the designers do not seem bothered at all.

As usual I had the Russian team. Just getting them to do anything is such hard work. A simple task, such as tightening up some nuts, took an hour and a half to two hours. No matter how many times I told them they were doing it wrong , they would go " yeah, yeah" , and then do it exactly the same again. I eventually got through to them and after about an hour and a half, in spite of them, not because of them, we got everything working. It may sound harsh but it's true. We would never employ any of them in the commercial world,. They don't seem to have any incentive to work and they lack initiative. They just don't understand about dumping hot water. I n these hot water suits if you get too hot , you either ask to have the temperature turned down or you dump the hot water from the suit I thought we had covered this with Vladimir but their divers are still having a problem. I get the impression that they're too scared to tell their supervisors that they're sick or ill or dehydrated with heat exhaustion. I am convinced they believe it's a sign of weakness and they work in an environment of you do not complain. A couple of them overheated again today and when they returned to the bell they were both very weak and exhausted. Phil the bell man told me that when they got back to the bell he could tell as soon as they took their hats off that they had heat exhaustion, both drank a litre of fluid straight off. When I informed Alexia the Russian supervisor his divers in a bad way he spoke to them to. But believe the divers won't admit they are exhausted. They reported everything's fine and there was no problems with the hot water. Tomorrow I'm try a different tact I will lower the water temperature and they will just have to ask me to raise it if they are cold hopefully this will work, I don't intend to go through this every day until someone collapses.

The grit cutter is just not performing nearly as well as NCA said it would It's just so bad it's unbelievable. It's going to cost a lot of time we're behind schedule now by quite a bit and we're not going to catch it up, no way. We're only going to drop further behind because of this cutter. We've spent the last three days trying to remove the first section of the outer hull, and that's just an inspection hole. The ironic thing is that the NCA guys don't appear to be embarrassed by it all. If I brought a piece of equipment out and said "This is the best gear there is. It'll do the job" and it then performed as badly as theirs is performing, at least I'd be bloody embarrassed about it. But they don't seem to give a damn. It can't even cut through the rubber, have they no sense of shame. We can't get on and do what we know we can do because the equipment is letting us down badly.

Another problem I'm encountering with the Russian divers is that, whereas our divers will stand by the hydraulic saw, touch it, lean on it, work with it; the Russians have to be five metres away from it. It's like they are approaching a time bomb. Everything has to be made cold (all the power has to be shut down) for them. Turn this off, we don't want to go near that, it's dangerous etc, its what we are hearing all the time. Even though they see our divers approach and work near by they insist there divers will not. We have assured them we will not ask their divers to perform any tasks that we would not ask our own divers to do. For me it's bloody frustrating because I have to supervise the Russian team and we must increase the productivity of the divers or the heat will be applied from above. What makes things harder is I can't even talk directly to the divers. I have to go via an interpreter then a Russian supervisor; I do not think what I ask for gets passed on to the divers?

The NCA brought on a couple of trouble shooters yesterday because they are undermanned and short of spares, they brought shed load of spares, and a couple of their bluest eyed technicians to help with the cutting machine, lets hope they have the magic that is required.

26th JULY

I am determined to say something positive about today. We removed our first outer hull section today, which creates our first glimpse of the pressure hull where we have to cut the coupons (holes for the lifting wires are installed). We also recovered one of the masts so that's two positive things. We have achieved some success with the cutting machine, not a lot but some. What else can I say that's positive? Not a lot really.

The mast which has the dome on top which I mentioned earlier is giving us a bit of a headache. Apparently its such a secret thing the Navy do not have the plans of what's inside, we asked the question for when dismantle it we did not want to damage any of its contents. The Navy said they would have to get in touch with the government owned company that installed it, apparently any maintenance or repairs required on this, a man from the company is dispatched to where ever she is berthed. The way we intended to remove this dome was by unbolting it this was not possible so the next plan was to burn of the mast and recover the dome plus a section of mast together. The problem we had with this method was, when we use a burning rig our burning medium is oxygen (o2) any excess o2 could egress into the *dome forming a large pocket of o2 which if ignited would create quite a big bang which could easily kill the diver. The Navy or Rubens the subs designers could not tell us what was inside the dome and we could not start until we knew, so we had to track down the company who installed it, we had to wait until the information was available to us. From asking the question 30hours passed before we got the go ahead to cut of the dome. If it's going to take that sort of time scale to get answers to our questions, we'll still be doing this in ten years time. Now we're busily hacking away at this thing now. It's ironic when you think of the time wasted on this dome, for to all intense and purpose it's a pile of scrap now, especially after we hacked away at it.*

I'm starting to get some overlap of work with the Brit team now (meaning I will run the British divers for part of my shift) it will be nice to talk to people direct, have them react and do the things you ask them to do without any big debates,; asking the admiral etc.. With a bit of luck the rotation might move round enough until I get the Brit team all the time. I live in hope.

While I was writing this I was unaware of goings-on elsewhere. According to Associated Press the chief Naval spokesman, Igor Dygalo was denying that the operation was running behind schedule (he obviously had not consulted the Admiral on the spot). In fact, he said, quite rightly, that the silt clearing work had proceeded very quickly. What he then went to say was chilling. The main fear was of a cable breaking during the lift, sending the "Kursk" crashing back down to the seabed or turning over. (The subsequent pollution dangers would be horrendous). Some experts, indeed, according to A.P. worried whether the two reactors could stand such shocks. But Nikolai Ponomaryov -Stepnoi, deputy chief of the Kurchatov Institute, Russia's leading nuclear research centre, had reassured doubters. He said, "All possible accidents had been studied and......... Experts concluded the reactors ....would remain safe".

27th JULY

What a twenty four hours we've just had! We recovered the masts and all their secret bits and pieces which they want to get off the boat a.s.a.p. We picked up the last piece, a small part of the periscope which we had to locate, during my last dive shift. So that'll all be taken off today, hidden away from the eyes of the world..

We're starting to work on one of the access hatches today. Progress is good and the grit cutter seems to be working fine. Touch wood! The relief divers are coming out tomorrow as we must start to decompress on the 29th to keep a rotation going. We intend to decompress one of the Russian teams. That will leave just the one Russian team. I'm afraid we'll just have to live with that (we would prefer to pull both Russian teams). The Russian Federation insisted that a Russian team shall remain in saturation; this is the first major confrontation between the Dutch and the Russians. The decision is made at a very high level onshore and the Russians win. The first crew change is on the 1st, via Murmansk, we believe. So the relief crew will fly to Kirkenes, spend the night there and travel overland to Murmansk, then helicopter out to the vessel from there.

I reckon that by the time I get up tomorrow 1st outer hull section will be up,(all the sections and debris we remove from the submarine will be stockpiled in designated areas on the sea-bed to eliminate any contamination of the ship plus we do not have the storage onboard). If that's the case then we're going to try and get stuck into the main hull. That could prove to be a very unpleasant job, as there is a possibility of coming across some bodies when we cut into the main hull. In Compartment five (the reactor compartment) there are thought to be some twenty bodies. If we find them it won't be a nice experience. I think it'll be a couple of days before we breach the pressure hull.

28th JULY

Quarter to eight in the morning and I've just finished shift. When I came on last night at six o'clock the Commander of the Northern Fleet Admiral Popov was on board. When a member of his entourage entered dive control with the commander a few paces behind I remarked "watch out lads looks like the top banana is here" referring to the Commander of the Northern fleet This officer in perfect English retorted "he's the biggest banana you will ever see" he sounded more English than me , It did take me back a bit. They brought with them what I can only describe as two very large jam tarts about 18inches diameter. We were informed that 29th was Navy day for the Northern Fleet and these tarts were traditional food eaten on this day. Because of the tragedy and as a mark of respect it would not be celebrated this year but they still wanted to present the team with the traditional food. To be honest these tarts had been travelling awhile and were not as fresh as they could be and were left to one side untouched, it was only when we were informed by the interpreter that these tarts had been baked by the women of the victims of the kursk to say thank you for what we doing for them. Knowing this made us feel very humble and brought home the enormousness of this tragedy and how many people are affected.   Because we're starting to get a bit complacent with what we're doing we've got to be careful and respectful. This job is fraught with risk it won't take much to turn this job into a second tragedy.

As far as work progress goes, we're getting on with cutter which is still not performing very well. The Russians have been Broccoing (Brocco is the name of a manufacturer which supplies the offshore industry with the best rods used for burning and cutting underwater this task is always referred to as Broccoing). When they have a Brocco gun in their hand they're happy We've needed to remove the upright supports between the hulls to release the first access hatch ,unfortunately the Russian divers are not to keen to enter into these areas where this work is performed, this task is exclusive to the British divers. We estimate the first outer section will be removed shortly which will be a good progress step. Another problem that keeps arising is the SMIT representative's keeps   sending us off to do other tasks, this very frustrating we would prefer to complete a task then move on to the next. We end up with lots of semi completed jobs and nothing finished. We are hopeful they will let us remain in compartment five to complete the first two holes in the pressure hull this would be a big sociological boost to the team which we need at this point in time.

We are performing a lot more Broccoing lately, far more than was envisaged before we left for this job. With the nature of burning underwater the unstable and unknown conditions of the Kursk it was risk assessed in Aberdeen and ruled it was to be kept to a minimum, the majority of the cutting would be performed remotely by the cutting machines. Judging by there performance to date that will not happen. The thoughts of the divers if there is to be any chance of success for this project we will be performing plenty of Broccoing, this of course will make this project that little bit more hazardous.

29th JULY

It's National Navy Day today and the Russians have been wishing themselves and us a Happy Navy Day. This entailed plenty of hugging back slapping and lots of smiling, due to the task we are performing the Russian northern Fleet commander has decreed there will be no celebrations this year as a mark of respect to there comrades of the Kursk.

We've been busily cutting away and have removed our first outer hull section from compartment five, we now have access to the void between the two hulls. This is where all the services for the submarine are installed, pipe work, winches, ballast tanks, and all utilities required by a Russian nuclear submarine. We have to remove vast amounts of this stuff before we can access the pressure hull.

The decision has been made as we expected it's the Russian to decompress the first team once they have completed their eight hour hold, (this is a hold prior to any decompression it lets the body stabilise and the O2 content is increased in the chamber) this will take four days to get the divers back to the surface. The Russian team have been nominated to be the first team to decompress which is the team I am running. There was plenty of political wrangling on which team was to be first out with the Dutch wanting all the Russian out and the Russian Federation resisting this. On a purely work rate decision it had to be the Russian out, and replaced by another British team, that benefits the project the most. The advantage to me personally is I will be working with an English speaking team with the same work ethic I am used to, no more disagreements with the Russians. I shall not miss waiting for the translating of every word, then the discussion of the merits or non merits of what was said, the work rate will definitely increase on my watch now.

The relief team who arrived yesterday was telling us about their horrendous journey, to get to the vessel. They incurred a five hour delay at the Norwegian/Russian border; the hotel in Murmansk was alright, with a bar and plenty of people to relieve them of their cash. The chopper pilots were excellent even though the helicopters themselves were a bit ropey. It was a journey they were not in a hurry to repeat again was the overriding opinion.

30th JULY

We had quite a productive night. I now had a British team, I didn't have any problem with translating etc. We've cleared out Compartment five (between the hulls) now, which gives us access to the pressure hull, we are ready to make our first breach into the inner hull of the submarine. We haven't cut the holes yet, but at least the cutting machine is getting more reliable by the day. We have to have special base plates to go onto the hull which fit in between the sub frames the cutter is then mounted on top of the base plates. The problem is they are not here yet and not expected to arrive no earlier than Wednesday. We are in a position now where we have cleared out compartment five and are ready to do the first lifting point holes, this will be another big milestone for the project. Because we can't continue in compartment five the decision has been made to continue with the outer section on compartment seven. I think we will be in a position to remove this section later on this morning. Once that is removed the divers will be back inside removing all the paraphernalia between the hulls, we have also made a start on removing the outer hull on section eight, productivity has picked up today.

The remaining Russians team did some brocco burning to-day, they had been working on a large section of the outer hull which had to be removed but it entailed a lot of burning there was one particular section which was very difficult to remove, but they were determined to remove this section before the end of their dive. Most uncharacteristically the supervisor let them run over their dive time to complete this task. When they had completed the final cut my team went in to remove the section, unfortunately it was not completely cut through which was fiercely denied by the Russian claiming we were lying to make them look bad, they are feeling a bit persecuted by the Dutch right now. They insisted that they would remain in the water until it was completed when they finished the cut my team removed the section, I was a little disappointed for the Russians they were so chuffed with their initial effort, but they did complete the cut so pride was restored. Roland (my fellow supervisor) did have to take the flak for running the team over there maximum dive time, he felt it was worth it to give his team a confidence boost and I agree.

One of the team was surfing the internet to-day and came across a CNN report stating that a chief naval spokesman for the Russian federation, Igor Dygalo denied accusations that the operation was running behind schedule. He must be looking at a different schedule from the one I'm working on, because I think we are well behind. We've got a lot of time make up to get back on the original schedule, and he doesn't mention anything about cutting off the front of the submarine. There is the transit time of the barge to include which is at least two days the setting up of the barge this all valuable time that is lost to the project. To-day we have had the pleasure of surveying the proposed cut line to release the front section of the submarine from the main body. The proposed cut line runs very close to the missile silos. The nearest silo to the cut has its outer hatch dislodged and the missile within is clearly visible. This did not seem to us as a problem until we were informed by the ordinance experts that the missiles are expelled from the submarine by a small gas canister from the base of the silo once the outer hatch is open, its only the natural buoyancy of the missile which brings it to the surface. Once the missile is near the surface a light sensitive cell kicks in and sends the missile on its way to its predetermined target be it London, Bonn Paris who knows. This was all very interesting to us and realised that we have to be careful until he added as a footnote to his monologue, that he believe the vibration of the cutting method we intended to employ to remove the nose section would be enough to set of the gas canisters and with the nearest silo's hatch dislodged we could send a missile on its way to were ever it is primed. This last statement grabbed our attention as you could imagine. I don't fancy being part responsible for destroying a major European capital.

31st JULY

The base plates for the pressure hull have arrived so we can now set up for cutting the first gripper hole(these are the holes in the pressure hull which will eventually contain the lifting mechanism which are called grippers). The big moment will soon be upon us. We were not set up until 0330hr we are now waiting for the word to start the first pressure hull cut, this will be into section five which is the nuclear reactor compartment we did not know what to expect whether a gas escape, water coolant from the reactor or any other type of escape. It's a tense moment; it appeared everyone is awake for this initial cut. According to Rubens design engineers for the Kursk, just below the first hole should be a ventilation duct nine inches in diameter, also they told us this was a station where five submariners would have been stationed when the accident occurred. We had to be prepared for the potential discovery of dead bodies, if this occurred protocol had been decreed that the Russian diver would deal with any bodies we may encountered, but with now only one team left in sat it would be very unlikely that they would be in the water when or if it happened, it was agreed if there were bodies we would cover the hole and wait until the Russian team are in the water to deal with it. It so happens that a high percentage of the British divers are ex military I myself having been stationed in Northern Ireland during the troubles as were others, the problem would not be as traumatic as it could be if you had never encountered a dead body before.

While we were waiting for the word we continued with the removal of the outer sections for compartments seven and eight, Smit tak seem very keen for us to start cutting the holes in the pressure hull, we all want to get cracking but they seem adamant that they want us to start cutting, until the Russians give the go ahead we can't. I have just found out that contractually Smit Tak will receive a stage payment when the first six holes are complete, I can see why they are so eager to get us cutting holes in the hull now.

A rather sensitive issue arose yesterday, the Admiral paid me a visit yesterday, because we have been working out in the gym most days together we have gained a bit of friendship we have a little bit of a rapport going on. He asked me what I thought of the Idea of splitting up the Russian divers, having a Russian working along side a Brit. I said it would be more problem than it was worth, I understand the work rate might go up but the communications would be unworkable and I expect the Russian diver would be side lined to fetcher and carrier. Unbeknownst to me the Dutch salvage master and my boss Sean had been on to him all day to split his one remaining team up, he used my argument to deny the request. Diplomacy not being my particular forte I suppose I should have kept me big gob shut, I did add it was only my opinion I don't think he mentioned that. Its 0600hr and the end of my shift I was hoping we would get the go ahead to start the cut by now, it will come just as I leave no doubt. Well we should have breached the pressure hull by the time I come on shift tomorrow.

NCA (the Norwegian cutting company) flew in one of their top boys today, he wanted to be present for the first pressure hull cut and to receive the flak for the cutting machines performances to date, I bet he wishes he didn't come now.

1ˢᵗ AUGUST

Crew change today and I've got to change shifts. I've got to start at mid-night which only gives me four hours kip before my next shift. They require me to change shift for continuity if we changed out shift for shift this would leave a situation of two supervisors on at the same time who have not been on the job yet, that would not be fair to them, there is quite a lot to get your head around. The down side for me is I will have to run the last Russian team, more translations and coaxing to contend with.

After my shift yesterday the word quickly came through for the go ahead to cut into the pressure hull, once we were through we had a massive escape of air which was expected. It continued to vent all day, when the submarine went down there would have been air trapped in the compartment which would have compressed with the depth, it's been venting all day so there must have been a lot. At about ten o'clock they continued with the cut. As I came off shift they were three quarters of the way round the first hole. Most of the night we were concentrating on Compartment seven and eight, removing the outer hull by burning and using the linear grit cutter The new method we have adopted is for the grit cutter to remove enough of the rubber so we can access the outer hull with a brocco rod then we will cut it by hand with the divers, this method has been forced on us as the cutting machine is not capable to cut all the way through the sonar rubber and the steel outer hull as claimed it could by the Norwegians. This method is extremely slower than we had scheduled for in the project, it made for a busy night for us.

I discovered a reason why permission was not granted early to start the pressure hull cut, they didn't want to start cutting in the early hours because all the top brass wanted to be awake to witness it. There was a bit of an altercation with the Russians about the marking up of the base plate positions for the first hole. The tolerance for the positioning of the base plates was 10mm; once the plate was positioned it was welded. We discovered the first plate was positioned wrong by the Russian divers, I have discovered there is no love lost between the Russian Federation Navy and the submarine designers Ruben ,Ruben were not best pleased about the mistake and stood over us like mother hens as we re-marked and position the base plate again. The second plate was only slightly out but acceptable after a long discussion with their bosses in St Petersburg. They claim that 10mm offset would jeopardise the lifting of a 10,000 ton submarine maybe we should not be trying to lift her in the first place. I asked the question about slippage which we are bound to get ,but engineers being engineers its all theoretical and its all calculated was their answer. Bollocks was my theoretical calculated reply.

2ⁿᵈ AUGUST

Half past one in the morning and I am well into my new shift, all the stories from the oncoming crew are filtering through their experiences in Mermansk the bus trip from Kirkines across the tundra and the now famous nickel plant they passed on the way. Apart from the few who were ripped of from the fair ladies of Murmansk, the sore heads from the drinking they mostly hated the journey.

3ʳᵈ AUGUST

We got the first coupon from 5:2 out(the coupon being the centre piece of the hole and 5:2 the compartment number and hole designated number in that compartment).   We had a bit of trouble with 5:1 because of the ventilation duct (as the Rubens engineers said it would, they got that right) was welded to the under side of the coupon. This Compartment had a possibility of five dead bodies inside it, though we never saw them. We took water samples for the radiation monitoring people, also a sample for the Russians so they could do their tests. Once we got the samples we tried to drop a camera inside but the visibility was to poor to see, we abandoned the videoing and installed a temporary cover over the hole.   Then we moved on to the next compartment, starting with the outer section, clearing away the debris and equipment between the hulls , then cut the pressure hull holes. It will be this routine for the foreseeable future.

We had a first re-supply this morning at three which went on through the night (even though this time of the year up here it's daytime all the time here!) Before we could back load (transfer equipment and stores from the re-supply vessel) we had to recover all our down lines and burning gear from the submarine. We were not permitted to back load while we were stationed over the submarine to reduce the possibility of a dropped object incidents. A container falling from the vessel and landing on the reactor Compartment was not a risk we were prepared to take. We need more washers and collets for the burning gear, we are getting desperately low as we did not envisage so much burning, hopefully they will arrive with these stores. We are also using up our supply of burning rods at a very rapid rate we are going to need a lot more than we thought, so much for the risk assessment in Aberdeen where no burning was the risk analysis outcome, it seems right now that's all we are doing.

4ᵗʰ AUGUST

We have now exposed Compartment seven we have got a lot of the burning to do here. There are seven high pressure cylinders inside We have to cut them out and dump them ,we have designated dump areas beside the submarine with the intent to clear this debris away at a later date. By the end of my shift we had managed to remove most of the large obstacles from the compartment. In Compartment eight there are some large ballast tanks we have to remove which will be tricky and take a lot of burning. By the end of tomorrow I think we'll have the equivalent of 11 holes ready for cutting on the hull itself, that's a lot more than I thought would be ready at this point in time, hopefully bulk of the so-called hard work, the heavy and large obstructions we need to remove is done. When we start on Compartment four, there are quite a few holes to be made there. I reckon if we get Compartment four done in two or three days then we're looking at making some serious headway. Of course it's all going to stop when the ATM Carrier (the cutting barge) arrives on site. We'll have to stand off while it does its mooring up and then the cutting of the front section phase will begin. The estimation is a week to ten days for the whole operation optimistic I think. We, of course, won't have access to the submarine during this phase as it will be a diver less operation with still unaccounted torpedo's down there and the small problem of the missile bay that the armaments expert eluded to earlier.

The Russian dive team on here are, in their normal military role an on-shore based team, and salvage is one of there expertise supposedly team. Their boss came on today, Alexander the interpreter was telling me he was one of the veteran divers who worked with the Russian special forces and was the most highly decorated serving diver, he had participated in the espionage game for real, he was considered a real hero by his team and was greeted very warmly with hugs and kissed from his men. I can't imagine that happening in the British forces when I was in.

5ᵗʰ AUGUST

Today's not been bad at all, I've had a bit of a laugh with the Russians, taking the mick out of each other, I keep offering them medals if they work harder, they intern let me know how good they are. Their boss man came into dive control to pay a visit to the coal face so to speak, he wanted to take photograph of their supervisors, Alexei the Russian supervisor or jaws as I nicknamed him(his teeth were dentures made of steel)insisted I was included in the picture, I must admit I did feel honoured. When the photograph was taken and we sat down Alexia said something and everyone looked at me and laughed waiting for Alexander to translate what he said,"I wanted you in the photo for the KGB who'll arrest you when you get to Murmansk". It did make me laugh it was the first real time their humour came through, and I am glad (well I hope its humour). We have completed another hole to-day that's three in total to date, plus another we just started cutting. We have another eight cleared and ready for marking up and base plate fitted, we are starting to make headway now. It's been slow progress but as we are gaining more access to the compartments progress is picking up. We are still encountering the problem of removing the coupons, because we are unable to gain access to the underside its hard to remove any of the pipe work or submarine structure welded to that side. All we can do is stick the crane onto them and try brute strength, if we are lucky they pull free sometimes we manage to get a big enough gap to burn of any problems. With the problems we are still facing and the ever present approach of the winter weather I still am not confidante that we will lift the Kursk this year, this could be just preparation for next year. This will prove that sanctimonious git from Halliburton who said it was an impossible task couldn't be done until next year. But we don't want to prove him right, do we?

We had a couple of the cutters working today, so that's good. I think once we get Compartment four is cleared out in the next week or so, there will be plenty of access to the pressure hull and we will catch up time. We heard on the grapevine that the trials performed on the ATM Carrier (the cutting barge) in Kirkenes failed, the diamond tipped cutting wire kept snapping. A different method has been devised, but due to the time restraints they will not have the time to re-test. The people at the top have decided to go with this untried method and will be sailing for the job site soon. We will have to move of location while the ATM Carrier (the cutting barge) sets up and cuts the front section off. I hope this new method works or it could prove the end of this project.

Smit Tak are working in a really crazy way - it's a fixed price job for them and they seem to be increasing their work instead of trying to decrease it. For instance, the dimensions for the guide cones for the grippers, which guide the lifting wires into the submarine, are too big, well over engineered.

This means we have to clear more area in between the hulls to install them. We want the dimensions decreased to cut down on the work involved to install them. Smit seem hell bent on increasing the dimensions which will give us a lot more clearance work. I know my company DSND are on day rate so if Smit want to mess about it's no great loss to us, but as a team we want to complete the salvage job this year for all those families who need us to do it and all those so called experts wrong who said it was impossible.

Dive control was paid another visit from the Head of the Russian Salvage Unit to-day you can see the respect is openly displayed for him by his team. I managed to have a chat with him via the interpreter and he gave me the impression of being old school but a very nice man. It would be interesting for him and Wally to have a chat, Wally was in our own special forces, SBS (Special Boat Service – the marine equivalent of the SAS) I bet they could tell some stories between them. A few years earlier they could have been in each others rifle sights trying to pop each other off. Funny old world.

6th AUGUST

Half past one in the morning. I'm knackered – just finished shift and been to the gym Today was quite a productive day. We've cut a couple of holes and there are another two ready to cut. I reckon by this time tomorrow we'll have at least seven holes completed. The Russians seem to be cottoning on to what we need from them now; which is good, we're getting some good work with them now. Pasha the second translator said to me that on the 12th, next week Admiral Popov the commander of the whole navy is coming and the hospital boat's going to return to port and pick up the families of those who perished on the "Kursk" to come and pay a visit to the site. That will be a year to the day since the terrible accident, they're coming out to pay their respects I am sure it will help with the grieving process. He believes they will be accompanied by the Head of the Northern Fleet and a sack full of government officials.

We have had word the ATM Carrier will be transiting to the site shortly its departure is imminent. We expect the tug boats to arrive tomorrow to lay the mooring anchors, they will then return to port to tow the barge out to the work site. I hope this barge can do what they say they it can, it's a big gamble if she fails to remove the front section its goodbye project, or at the least so much lost time we would have to abandon the project until next year.

I was a very pissed off today, one of the Smit representatives was trying to give our divers a bit of grief. The divers made a cock-up, I'm not trying to defend that sometimes it happens. This guy have jumped on his high horse and berated these two divers. These are the same two divers who are pulling Smit out of the shit by making do with inadequate gear, burning far more than was ever intended, and going deep into the submarine to cut the outer hull supports to save using the cutting gear which is very slow, and if that's not enough they are working harder to compensate for the less experienced Russians and yet this arse hole has the nerve to give us grief. All because of a mix up with a measurement, which meant one extra cut to remove a section of pipe. Sometimes they should engage brain before operating mouth. On a lighter subject I have been wagering with the cutting company (NCA), the bet with their boss is whether they can cut a hole in the pressure hull, in one go they have not managed it yet. The problem they have is leaving small bridges which have to be re-cut. Every time they fail it's a free T shirt for me, Ill be able to open a market stall by the time I get back to UK. I may not take the bet much more though they are getting closer every time. I don't have any T shirts to play with.

7th AUGUST

It's been a good day today. We got three coupons out in Compartment eight that completes that compartment for holes in the pressure hull, we have just been informed by the designer of the grippers which will be inserted into the hole for the lift, that we have to clear an area on the under side of the hole. These grippers once they are inserted into the hole 300mm approx have two feet witch are hydraulically activated once inside the hole, these feet will rest on the submarines structural frames this is were the weight of the submarine will be taken. For this to be successful the contact area has to be clear of any obstruction, we have been given a tolerance of 5mm. This creates problems for us the main one is when we are burning we use O2(oxygen) this can build up in this confined space and if it ignites we have our self's a big explosion. The other problem is access to these areas we are not allowed into the submarine so it would mean hanging upside down and trying to burn at the same time. It will also increase the work load when we are doing our best to decrease that. On the inside of the submarine where the holes are situated there are all sorts of objects   the biggest headache so far is the corner of a bomb blast door, very heavy steel, it needs removing that going to give us problems. At this moment in time we are concentrating on removing the sonar buoy doors in Compartment four, these are to massive hydraulic doors which when at sea they can open them up and release a sonar buoy on a winch for communications and spying. The swing arms on these doors are massive and we have to not only cut them free but then manhandle them out of the submarine, we have been at it a few hours already. The Russians had a good dive today and they were watched by the next Russian team who will replace them, they do seem very nice blokes but are very inexperienced in this kind of work, I am sure if we needed a mine de-fusing they would be ideal, but not for the work we require them to do. The Admiral paid us a visit to-day he was very interested in how we extracted the coupons, which is brute strength and luck. He insisted on giving me some more naval badges to add to my ever growing collection. After he left Vladimir came into dive control(A Russian dive supervisor) he had just returned from 7 days of leave it was nice to see him again, he was given the leave pass because it was his birthday. He told me spent a whole month's salary in one weekend about $300 dollars, all of it on vodka.

I also had a very interesting conversation with the interpreter , the news was all about the incident when the Russian Deputy prime Minister was visiting with some of the relatives of the disaster and a mother of one of the crew was shouting at him hysterically which was being filmed for the worlds media. In full view of the cameras a so called nurse injected her in the neck to sedate her. He did agree she was drugged to quieten her down, but he argued that the doctors were standing by for they expected some of the relatives would be over ought and needed help. I said that's one perspective another is she was embarrassing him and they did what ever it took to shut her up. He did agree it was not a good idea to do it while the world press was watching.

We're surrounded by ships, more than usual and no one can tell me why, we are expecting the Tug boats which will position the anchors for the ATM Carrier (the cutting barge) to-day I do not think that would be the reason. I think they just like to out number us.

8th AUGUST

Quite an eventful day today. We removed another three coupons, we've now got 5.1, 5.2, 8.1, 8.2, 8.3, 7.4, 7.5, 7.1, 7.2. That's nine coupons out now. The coupon extraction count will slow down drastically if not halt altogether now because we have to concentrate on the removal of the outer hull sections for compartment four this is the biggest compartment for the lifting holes, and there is plenty of obstructions to remove in between the hulls. My team was given the task of continue with the removal of the masts to-day because the submarine will be eventually lifted up under a barge, we have to remove them or we would pierce the hull of the barge as we lifted. They have to be cut back to a maximum height of 380mm. the method we will use is a hydraulic operated saw which we hope will cut through with no problems, its a proven method so as long as the masts are not made of same r steel should be no problem we managed with the mast with secret dome on so it should be ok..

I talked to some of our guys who came out of "sat" yesterday. They had been tasked to survey the proposed cut line for the front section removal. Both divers thought that the point where the intended cut line was not good, they had seen a better site were a large crack which extended to the seabed was a much better site as the cut would be 80% through before you even start. The obvious advantage to the project if this was true is only a small amount of cutting will be required from the ATM Carrier reducing the time on site considerately.

The Russian team are now getting quite confident it is reflecting in their work output, unfortunately now that they are getting the hang of it, they will be the next team to decompress in about 5 days time. The word is that they will not be replaced with Russians. As you can imagine this is not going down to well with the Russian navy, they have taken this decision to the highest levels on shore and are waiting for a reply. They seem very confident this decision will be overturned and they will prevail, I am not so sure, it makes more sense to me to replace them with another British team and up the work rate to full potential. I have to admit though these Russian divers have worked very hard, they dived every day, six hours in the water with no real complaints 10 out of 10 for effort. I expect the media still think it's the Russians and Dutch doing all the work and now it will soon be all Brits.

9th AUGUST

It's been a long old day today. Compartment IV is open we managed to get those massive doors out it seem to take for ever. Now with the compartment laid bare to us we can see the sonar array in all its glory it look like a massive black bomb the type they used to drop during the second world war. We still had more of the outer hull to remove to gain access to the pressure hull hole positions this compartment will be home for 10 holes. My Russian team was tasked to survey the holes we had cut so far, when a hole was cut we immediately covered the with a wooden cover to keep everything inside i.e. stop bodies from floating out. The task was officially to see if we had any internal obstacles to remove but unofficially it was to see if any bodies were going to be in the way when we started working on the holes. I was very tense with this , we would be informed on what to expect for example one hole was directly above a bunk bed we knew this from the designers who had all the lay outs of the decks. We were warned of possible bodies in this location 2 or maybe 3. I was a bit nervous when we looked into that hole, we clearly saw the beds but no bodies thank god. We were very lucky we did not come across any bodies during the survey. We did find some obstacles that will need to be removed, mostly pipe work and a few electrical cabinets nothing to bad so far.

We had a request for another survey of the proposed cut line for the removal of the front section to-day from the cutting experts on the barge. It's quite hard to explain how they intend to cut this section off, ill try. There will be two suction anchors either side of the front section where the proposed cut is, between them will be a diamond studded wire (industrial diamonds yes we did think about it) the wire was laid out over the submarine. With a system of sheaves this wire was attached to winches on the barge deck, the winches will then pull the wire back and forth like a saw. The sheaves are reeved so a downward pressure will be applied onto the submarines hull, so many tons of pressure will be required to move the wire back and forth as it cuts through the hull 20ton or more. Eventually when the pressure drops of the winches this will indicate that its cut all the way through the submarine. If this can be performed with no diver intervention that will be great but I doubt it. Sunday will be the day of reckoning when the barge arrives.

The latest gossip we are chewing over right now is the next crew change(we are like old women sometimes) off going crew has to wait for their relief's because bad weather in Murmansk, the helicopters have been grounded, they decided to crew change by boat. The oncoming crew will be transported by fast patrol boat, the estimated time is 15 hours that's a long time in a fast patrol boat.

Since I last wrote the relief crew has arrived and they look like a bunch of drowned cats, looking very pale. It turned out when they arrived at the dock there was this very ropey looking boat they we told to board, they were not too keen but were tempted with the bait of," this will only transport you too the Admiral's launch which will take you the rest of the way". It was true there was the Admiral's launch waiting for them but it was not much better than the vessel they were already on. When they eventually arrived at the site, the cries of never again, and do not go on that boat to the off going crew was very funny to all who were not crew changing, the oncoming crew was telling anyone who would listen how outrages this is. I did not envy them this particular journey, and the little consolation is that this method of crew change will not be adopted again.

The topic of the guide cones which align the grippers into the hole we have cut into the pressure hull raised its ugly head again to-day the onshore engineers insist they want to make them bigger while we wish them to be smaller to save us the extra clearance work that would be required. I believe a compromise is within our grasp. We had a minor incident to-day when the divers were in the water we lost all communication lights and cameras I don't think the divers new much about it but the Russian supervisors were concerned, it something that happens every now and then, the electrical technician soon repaired the problem and we carried on.

10th August

Once we complete this cut that will give us a grand total of eleven, this will be another stage payment for Smit and Mammoet 40% of the total cost will have to paid when we complete this hole. Good news on the gripper guides they appeared to have come to there senses and agreed to reduce the size, which will hopefully reduce the preparation time. Four weeks ago I had my doubts about completed the salvage this year, but with the latest efforts of everybody I think we can as long as the ATM Carrier performs as it should. We were hoping to have all 26 holes completed by the end of the month, but with the barge elbowing us out of the way for at least ten days it's looking doubtful.

By this time tomorrow we will have eleven holes cut, and with luck we will have compartment four cleared ready for cutting the hull holes. We have been asked to re-measure the masts the tolerance has been reduced to none now we will have to trim them again, re-doing work not a good idea. We have received some photo's to-day of the grippers which we will have to install, I did not imagine them to be so big they weigh 4 tons each, the photo's were accompanied with some photo's of the guides they seem even bigger I do hope they are not as big when they get here.

A new team was blown into "sat" tonight and we had to start decompressing one of our better teams, Stevie Upwood and co. Shame we couldn't keep them in for the whole job, a very good team, but they done their time we must decompress them now. When a new team replaces them they have to learn the ins and out of the job, they got to familiarise themselves with the work which takes time, *they do have the advantage of seeing the equipments working as it should, and to ask questions of the operators.*

I am getting on very well with the Russians now, we seem to understand each others humour now, as a team they are very touchy feely, always hugging and kissing each other when they meet even I am getting the odd embrace which to us tight arsed British tradition is not macho. But I think with this is an indication of acceptance, which is good.

I reckon by the end of tonight we'll have finished Compartments V, VIII and possibly VII as well, we will then concentrate on compartment IV, progress is very good now. It's looking better all the time we could do this yet.

11th AUGUST

Two o'clock in the morning, just finished shift and it's been quite an eventful day. Smit has presented us with our bonus for extracting eleven coupons out they receive a payment of 40% the project, they give us some sweets. We have actually removed twelve coupons and cracking on with compartment IV we have also had a look at compartment III there are two sections to compartment III one each side of the conning tower close by the silo's. I think these will give us some problems not as big an area to work on at these points of the submarine. One big plus though is the compartments that are left are close together so there is not as much shifting equipment about the submarine, Its been like working on a football pitch with one compartment on the goal line the next on the centre line and we have to keep moving equipment from one to the other, The last two sections are at least in the same 18 yard box. We had a stores delivery to-day we needed more breathing mix and O2 for the chambers. We were paid a visit by the camera crew who are making the documentary I managed to have a little chat with the producer he told me he was offered 100,000 guilders for a photograph of the Kursk. For that kind of money I said ill give him as many as he wanted, it shows how we are so isolated from the media interest.

Tomorrow Sunday12th, there's going to be a minute's silence for the anniversary of the disaster. I think it was 11-something when it went down. The Russians have written a memorial scroll which is sealed in a container and it will be placed inside the "Kursk" during the minute's silence. It's obvious it will bea moving moment for them, especially as the families are to attend from the hospital ship. I must say that my respect goes out to Seven who organised the flowers for the ceremony, Smit were not too fussed. They said it is normal to work on salvage sites with bodies inside, which I thought was rather heartless.

Smit are trying to delay the cutting off of the forward Compartment because the weather forecast is not very good for the next week, this will work in our favour as it will give us more time on the submarine we are on a bit of a roll right now with compartment IV. If we have another eight days we think we could be nearly finished. If we can finish before the ATM Carrier starts to get in position, while its doing its thing we could run to Kirkenes and offload the cutting equipment it will not be required again , we are also due a crew change which we could do along side which is always preferred.

I received some gifts to-day from ASC (the Dutch radiation monitoring team). They dished out some T-shirts and baseball caps that their company had made especially for us. They were printed with "Kursk Salvage Team 2001" so we are trying to embarrass Smit into sending us some similar. Not much chance from our own company "don't want to dent profits".

My dive team had a day off today because the timing of the stores transfer the stores transfer was to coincide with their time in the water because they are the least productive. I have asked Vassili (one of the designers who work for Ruben) if he would get some stamps for my daughter when he goes on leave, he is due off to-day for a week I offered to give him some money but he said "no not required". I know they are not the most well paid people in the world so ill settle up with him when he returns. I also heard a rumour that a medal will be made for the salvage team, I expect it will be for the naval personnel involved. I can't see the likes of us receiving anything. .

12th AUGUST

It's quarter to two in the morning shift over; we've had a fairly constructive day. The sonar doors which we were removing earlier caused us problems. We remove one door but thought the second would not interfere with the positioning of the holes it would be nice to remove but not required, as it transpires it does, and we have to remove it. Smit have been giving us grief about it they don't need much excuse to get at us, we mainly ignore them when they get like that. We eventually managed to get the second door out without the help of our intrepid Smit rep. We had a telling of to-day from the Russians for wandering down to the propeller area of the submarine apparently this is a top secret area they are very anxious for us not to see, it was reiterated in no uncertain terms that we must not go there. During my dive with the Russian team yesterday we had a good look around for a place to put the scroll that the Russian have put together for the ceremony later to-day we decided to place the scroll which was encased in a water tight brass container in the front of the conning tower. The Russian dive team had composed the written text on the scroll and since I had the honour of being involved in the placement ceremony I asked Alex the interpreter if he would read me what was written. A rough translation was they vowed to recover this scroll when the Kursk was transported to the dry dock and all the bodies had been repatriated to Russia soil. I asked if I could have a copy for myself which they obliged.

We managed to get a little look into compartment III this morning and it is full of equipment and pipe work which will have to be removed, its the most full compartment to date, we are having trouble getting access to the underside of the outer hull to remove the girders holding it in place they will need cutting before we can remove the outer hull. I think we are considering ripping the outer hull off with the vessel crane we have to careful there if we break the crane its goodbye project. The new designs for the gripper guide cones arrived to-day it looks like they have heeded our warnings they are smaller in design. Right now we are racing against the ATM Carrier; we need to do as much as we can before they ask us to move over.

The Deputy of the Northern Fleet is due any time now to attend the remembrance ceremony, it was going to be the commander Admiral Popov but he is now going to attend the ceremony in Murmansk with the families and relatives of the victims who were originally going to fly out but the weather would not permit this.

Its now Quarter to twelve in the morning and we've just had the ceremony of remembrance for the tragedy of the "Kursk". I thought it was a very moving experience, we were gathered on the heli deck in front a large Russian helicopter, the Vice Admiral of the Fleet who was representing the Russian Federation made some speeches which was simultaneously translated then at the precious moment of the tragedy the ships horn blasted which was taken up by all the vessels surrounding. We all had carnations which we threw into the water while a especially composed Lamont was played. After that there were some presentations of books to the heads of each company represented on the project. I was told these books were written by prominent Russians giving their own tributes to the victims leading poets and authors as well as biographies of the lost souls who were only 116metres below us. The scroll was presented to us for placement later on in the day with the word that it will no be retrieved until the crew are returned to port. All this was recorded for the Russian TV networks I hope someone gets comfort from this.

13th AUGUST

It's now two o'clock in the morning; I am still in a shock during the dive we were tasked with clearing out compartment five and at the same time start the cutting on the outer hull for compartment III. At 23:27 preciously, we were working on the submarine one diver Sparky was in the middle of re-positioning the cutter on compartment III, the second diver Gordon was about to unhook the crane from a load on the sea bed, the cutting team had just started cutting a hole No4:7 in the pressure hull in compartment IV. There was a massive explosion which shook theour vessel, my first reaction was to look at the divers cameras to see if we still had pictures at the same time both divers screamed. My first thought was a torpedo had gone up, luckily our drills kicked in, the bellman started to prepare for a rescue, both diver responded to my voice confirming that they were ok and responsive. We immediately recovered the divers to the bell without incident unsure if any more explosions would occur, when the diver were in the bell we recovered them to the surface it was the quickest recovery of all time, it goes to show all those drills we do all the time came into there own then. When we were on surface and everything had settled down we had a post-mortem on the incident. Rubens the submarine engineers insisted that this area we were working in was above accommodation there should not be anything explosive in the area they showed us photo's to prove this fact. The only intrusive work was undertaken at the time was the cutting of the 4:7 hole this method of cutting was employed because its classed as a cold cut, but some heat is still generated at the tip on the high pressure nozzle, this could be enough to ignite any explosive gas that may have been trapped in the compartment. After reviewing the video tape of the hole cut, I could not see any indication of ignition of gas with the nozzle. Up to the point of the explosion the machine was cutting as normal, when the explosion happened the machine just fell over no rush of gas out of the cut which is what you would expect. I don not think the cutter ignited anything and the cutter operator agrees with me, which begs the question what happened. Smit were trying to play down the incident I am sure if the media got a hold of this it could jeopardise the project. As a team this was not our concern, just the safety of the divers and of course the ship and crew, if a big enough explosion occurs and the gas bubble it could create came up under the ship it could sink her. It was not reported to the press for fear of the bad publicity it would attract and possible calls for work to cease on the project. After completing a medical examination of the divers we agreed no harm was done. We sent down the work class ROV to investigate the work site, everything looked normal. This has been reported to the highest levels and we are on stand bye until the boffins come up with some idea what happened. I am racking my brains to think what it could be, the size of the explosion makes me err on the side of military type explosives but I am not sure. All work has been stopped apparently the insurance company who is underwriting the project has a clause about explosions going off, If the insurance is withdrawn that will end the project for sure. For all you superstitious people out there it was the 13th day, it was the 13 hole we were cutting and exactly a year to the day of the tragedy.

To add to our woe's we had a newspaper article faxed to the vessel from Holland, obviously all in Dutch but when it was translated, it reported that a section of the last off going crew was severely criticising the Russians and Dutch complaining about how inept they were and that there is no chance of the Kursk being raised this year. The Dutch are going berserk about this and want the men fired never to return to the vessel, the Russians are not to pleased either, this is what you would call a diplomatic incident. Our boss contacted the accused to get their version of what happened, which was nothing like what was reported. They said four Dutch reporters practically abducted them, were very aggressive in questioning them. When no reply was forthwith they reported what they wanted with total disregard for the truth, It almost makes me sympathetic to the celebrities when they have stories reported about them with no truth involved if they would do it to a couple of divers. It took some persuasion to convince Smit that this was the case, and they relented in seeking retribution against the accused.

The Commander of the Russian Navy is supposed to pay us visit to-day, remember I mentioned the books that were presented to the company representatives during the remembrance ceremony. Well we had been all promised a copy of the book and to-day he was going to bring them. I hope I manage to get a copy I want to get everybody on the project to autograph the cover as a keep sake.

I heard that the barge for cutting off the forward Compartment has got a problem with its hydraulics or something. They're working on it but it's a delay and that will give us a bit more time to try and complete the holes before it can be repaired.

As I mentioned earlier I have a copy of the scroll that was placed in the front section of the conning tower, I also have a copy of the video of the placing of the scroll. Sods law though as we were about to place the scroll, it slipped from his grasp so there is a bit unscripted fumbling about but he got there in the end. When the scroll was in place the divers stood to attention on the submarine and saluted it was a very moving site. Let's hope we can keep the promise made in the scroll and bring them back home.

14th AUGUST

Half past twelve in the morning as I go on we are still awaiting the results of the conferences that went on between the Dutch, Russians and British about the explosion, what was the probable cause and what are the safety implications? Is what we want to know. One theory offered is when the submarine is submerged it has to make its own oxygen by extracting it from water and the by-product of this is hydrogen, this highly flammable gas is stored in cylinders in the submarine and disposed of when it surfaces. The theory continues that one or more of these cylinders ruptured during the tragedy ant the hydrogen escaped and formed a pocket in compartment IV and it was the cutter that ignited the gas when it was cutting hole No 4:7. That's the only plausible explanation they've come up with to date. After a lot of to-ing and fro-ing and talking, it was agreed that we could go back in to complete the coupon that we were cutting. We re-set the cutter to finish the cut then recovered the divers to the surface as a precaution. When the cut was completed without incident, we sent the divers back in to recover the coupon. The coupon was removed; we took water samples for analysis and also employed a remote camera to inspect inside the Compartment to see if we could confirm the explanation given for the explosion. We were unable to prove or disprove the theory because of the very poor visibility inside the Compartment. Our confidence in the safety of the project was shaken now, could there be any more of these pockets may be much bigger? Who knows? I am still not convinced that the cause has been explained, but with no other theory to go on we just have to be more careful. I believe we'll just carry on now, there's not much else we can do. It's either carry on or stop the job and I don't think that will be an option just yet. With all this carry on a delegation from the crew was organised to ask for our company (DSND) to at least recognise the fact that this is not an ordinary job as they proclaim but it is dangerous.

We had a visit from a Russian tug to-day to remove what debris we had recovered to deck, the Russian are responsible for any nuclear waste disposal. All the material on the job has been designated as nuclear waste for the purpose of disposal. I am not sure where its going but right now its sailing away on a tug to where ever, I did not see the crew of the tug wearing any kind of protective equipment when handling this stuff ?.

15ᵗʰ AUGUST

Two o'clock in the morning, we are concentrating on Compartments IV, III. The outer hull of compartment III is giving is grief its difficult removing the support brackets and brute force is being met with some resistance. We had to take a lot of measurement checks to-day for the gripper guides, as we expected the size of the guides will entail more clearing out between the hulls for them to fit. We are still getting backlash from the article in the Dutch papers, Smit (who are Dutch) still want to sack the divers involved (who are British). The divers are being backed by Wally and he will defend them, which will hopefully keep them their jobs.

A bond has been formed with me and the Russian team now, a new team was blown in to-day to replace my Russian team. I now have Vladimir Dimitri and Dave as the British member as the bellman, the bellman will remain in the bell for the whole dive and monitor the gasses and be prepared for any emergency recoveries that he may be called upon to do. He is tasked to be the bellman every time which is not normal the divers usually rotate themselves daily. It was their first dive to-day they reached the job site ok managed some work and got back, that's the main thing. Just need to keep it up for the next 28 days and everything will be great.

16ᵗʰ AUGUST

Half past two in the morning. It's been a long day of burning and more burning. We did the last of the rubber cuts today, we can dispense with the linear cutter which is a big relief for the divers. The sonar rubber is cut on the outer hull of compartment III but we still have to remove the steel hull section which is proving difficult. We have been burning massive amounts of steel in compartment IV it seem constant burning 24/7. We believe hole 4:9 will be attempted tomorrow this we believe is the highest point of the submarine that we will be breaking into, if there is going to be an explosive gas pocket this is where it will be. For safety reasons we not attempt this cut while there are divers in the water we will monitor the cut with an ROV, if this one cuts without incident this should give us a straight run until the end There was another delay on the barge announced today, I am not sure when it's coming now. There was a crew change today so the lads went off and a new crew came aboard. They're a couple of new lads that I did not know I think their Dutch. I was also very surprised that the oncoming crew had not been informed about the explosion we had below. Everyone on this job is a volunteer but it's only right the facts must be put to them for them to make an informed choice. I think this is all about playing the incident down and not wanting the press to get a hold of the story.

I had a laugh and joke with the Admiral today when he popped in to see us, even with the language barrier we still could communicate. The Russian team did their second dive today, they're still finding their feet but they're doing alright.

17th AUGUST

Its two minutes past two. It's been a very trying day today, very trying indeed. A lot of problems with the dives, mostly with the reclaim (The reclaim is a system of returning the exhaled gas from the divers to the surface where it is cleaned, scrubbed and heat treated to kill bugs, oxygen is then added to make it life sustainable again it is then sent back down to the divers) if we did not employ this system we could not carry enough gas to last a couple of days instead of the many weeks we have to stay on a project. They say the gas in saturation has passed through the bodies of many divers many times, make you think doesn't it. With the Russians dive we tend to loose a lot more gas than when the British dive, there can be many reasons for this, it could be leaks in the system hats not working properly. But unfortunately when the next team follow them who at are British they do loose nearly as much gas, we can not sustain this amount of loss for very long. We can only carry a limited amount for the replenishment, the gas is also required for the compression of the chambers when a new team is blown into sat, the lock runs and many other small things which all adds up, always closely monitored the gas figures are updated daily.

I finished shift we had completed the removal of coupon 4:9 and were close to finishing 4:10 progress is not as fast as everyone would like but we are getting there. The Russians have cornered me and asked me to explain to them why the reclaim issue only affects them. I think the Dutch are using this as ammunition for there argument for pulling their last team out of sat. I think we have come this far with the Russians we should persevere, after all it is their countrymen down there and its a Russian submarine I think its not only a question of pride but honour as well. The down side to them pulling the Russians is they want to replace them with Dutch people who have only just completed their saturation course, this is not the time to go into your first sat. They will definitely struggle when they see us working they tend to forget that we had been at this game 20 years plus. This is diplomatic they want to have Dutch divers on the job not only because its the biggest profile job ever, its run by Smit supposedly the biggest and best salvage company in the world, but also they have told the worlds press that Dutch divers are doing the work. If the Dutch get their way it will mess the rota up its very important to keep the rota going because it takes so long for decompression that some divers will be in a situation where they need to be on their way out but no chambers available. The Dutch are really pushing for this, we will find out who's really pulling the strings on this job soon.

It's Alex's the translators birthday tomorrow, Pasha who covers the night shift translating told us he was 50. I made a card for him and the cook baked him a cake when Pasha saw what we had planned for him he started to backtrack about how old he was, claiming he only thinks he's fifty. When we see his face tomorrow we will know if it's right or not.

We had a slip-up on one of the base plates today. On 4:10 we didn't position it up far enough. This affected the next cut so we had to go back and re-do it. The Dutch were a bit pissed off about that - a bit more ammo against the Russian Federation divers. In my opinion there's no way they are going to get the Russian divers out of there for the Dutch boys - it just doesn't warrant it - and I don't think the Russians will let them anyway. After all The Russians is the main client.

18th AUGUST

.It's early morning - one o'clock. A lot of burning today, as usual. We cut 4:5 but it needs pulling out, it's well jammed inside we will get the crane on it later and give it a tug. We are cutting 4:6 now we are slowly approaching 26 holes. Tomorrow we've got nineteen journalists coming on board to see

what's been happening. They're supposed to be coming early in the morning I think it's "get' them on get' them off" sort of routine as quickly as possible.

Guess what – we had our little birthday for Alex to-day we had a big gathering in the mess, I gave him his card and we presented him with a very ornate birthday cake curtsey of the chef. You could tell he was very moved by our display of affection for him so I thought. He made a speech and thanked us all told us to get stuck into the cake , he said it did not matter that he was only 49 we all stared at Pasher.

We had more problems with the reclaim; we were loosing a lot of gas on our dive. The Dutch ever the opportunist complained about the Russians again, we got it sorted and everything was fine from then on. To-day is Saturday a target has been set to finish the holes by Wednesday this would mean removing three coupons tomorrow and another two the day after, it's a tall order and I don't think we have much chance of finishing by them. I would gladly eat my words on that if I have too, but there is still a lot of debris and equipment to remove just to access the pressure hull for the hole cutting. I think we will be doing good if we have the preparation work completed leaving the holes. As I mentioned before if we are finished we can sail to port offload the cutting gear and pick up the dreaded gripper guides.

19ᵗʰ AUGUST

It's half past one, we have been busy, and we had a delivery of stores which we took onboard. We have completed hole 4:6 and started 4:7 we are doing well. I watched the discovery channel earlier it showed a documentary about the sinking of the Kursk, the conclusion it came to was the fuel used for the propulsion of the torpedo's was believed to be hydrogen peroxide. When this fuel comes in contact with metal it expands at a colossal rate which is the same definition of an explosion a rapid expansion of gas. The theory proposed by the programme was the fuel line to the torpedo about to be launched was cracked and the fuel leakage is what caused the initial explosion, this caused the ignition of the remainder racked torpedos. This they reported explained the small initial explosion recorded by the seismic station in Norway followed by the much larger explosion of the remaining torpedos. When I was watching this programme next to me was an Russian engineer from Rubin as we watched the programme I was doing my best to explain what they was saying, he was very interested in the torpedo compartment when it was shown on the programme. Later when I had the opportunity to explain the theory proposed by the programme with the help on the interpreter, I asked what his response was. He said he had heard about the hydrogen peroxide theory but discounted this with the explanation that the fuel used was not what they said, but did not elaborate on what it was.

The first Russian "sat" team arrived on surface today; it was like the return of the conquering hero's. The Admiral and many of the Russian team were waiting outside the chamber the divers were greeted with bear hugs and kisses from all who gathered to witness there return to the surface. It was obvious to me some how they had sneaked some vodka into them and was quite upbeat. Later Andre(one of the divers from the team) presented me with a bottle of Vodka which had his picture on the label dressed in full diving gear, he told me he had a friend who had a factory which produced Vodka and he commissioned 300 bottles with his picture on the label and called it Deep Sea Diver vodka. This I shall keep for a long time, mainly because of the story, secondly it looked like rocket fuel and would most probably kill me if I drank it. I asked if he would take it back and get the whole team to autograph the label for me as a keepsake.

The weather forecast is not good for us it is predicting a storm, 55knot winds are heading our way we have been lucky with the weather to date the Barent sea is renowned for its gales and rough seas. We are in a lull right now but we will be hit hard later in the day we can dive in pretty rough weather but the prediction is we will have to pull of. This decision has to be taken well in advance of the sea state becoming to rough to dive, because we have to recover all the equipment on the submarine recover the divers and position the vessel to take the weather full on.

I have not been to happy to-day, I have had a confrontation with the Russians everything I asked them to do to-day has been met with resistance. It's been either denied or we have to clear it with the Admiral or it's too dangerous. I must have been in a bit of a downer myself to-day because normally I would overcome such problems with a laugh and a joke but not this time. I told them to get their act together and do what you are here to do and stop pissing about. I was not the usual happy go lucky chap and they realised this the next few hours were a little strained but I managed to buck myself up apologised to them, we are all friends again you can't afford to fall out on a job like this we have enough problems with the job it's self let alone squabbling We managed to put the press of again due to bad weather I think the may get the impression that they are not welcomed here now, Tuesday is the new date for their arrival.

20th AUGUST

It's twenty to one in the morning, the weather did what was predicted and peaked at 50 knots which picked the sea state up to a level where we could not dive. We were delegated a 10 square mile area by the Russian and told to remain in this area until the weather subsides. The wind dropped of to 38 knots but the sea state remained up. There we were confined to our area to ride out the storm while the pride of the Russian navy ran for cover. So much for our security cordon! But there were a lot of sea sick people onboard.

21st AUGUST

Most of yesterday was lost to weather we managed to get back in the water at 1500hrs , we deliberately timed if for the Russian team to dive knowing that they are not as willing to work between the hulls as the Brits. Because the weather was still a bit rough we kept our work to the outer sections of the submarine. We concentrated with the outer sections to be removed from compartment III the sonar rubber has been cut its a matter of getting access to cut the steel plate and supports, unfortunately we had problems with one of our Brocco burning torches and we are now down to one this will slow us up.. The next team went about half-nine and they are setting up for cutting in the circle on 4:6 and then will transfer over to 4:5 which is ready to go. Hopefully they'll get those two done during the night. We will then concentrate our burning efforts all on compartment III, we have had glimpses of what lies below the outer hulls of compartments III there are two area one either side of the conning tower, there are masses of pipe work and ballast tanks. I think these two sections are going to give us the most problems; this area was the closest to the blast. We have been given a new completion target for the holes of a week; we will be doing well if we can manage that. There is a good incentive for us not only a crew change along side but the possibility of a run ashore for the crew. NCA will be able to go home in the knowledge that they completed their task successfully even though it was not quite to plan.

73

The weather forecast is not good. We need it better than this if we are to stand a chance of completing on time. A couple of guys are supposed to be going off today but I don't think we'll get any choppers if the weather stays like this, they are going to be on for an extra day at least.

I mentioned about the vodka bottle presented to me from one of the Russian divers Andre, I asked if he could get the divers to sign it for me. He re-presented it to me to-day but instead of signing the bottle they had attached a signed photograph of the Kursk as she was about to set of on her maiden voyage. I am very chuffed about this, its something I will always treasure.

22nd AUGUST

We lost more time to the weather and was standing by waiting for the sea state to come down so we can get back in the water working. It started to drop early evening and we got the go ahead to dive at 2200hrs, we need to make some progress on compartment III and get compartment IV cleared.

We found out today that a political decision has been made to put a single Dutchman into "sat"; we believe it's purely political. This will enable Smit to claim the Dutch divers recovered the "Kursk". I was surprised that the Russians did not give them more of a fight. I know they did not want this to happen. I discovered that the decision had to be taken at the highest levels for the Russian team on the boat to accept, it went all the way to Moscow and finally there resistance gave way to an uncomfortable acceptance. I think the Russians in Moscow are being very clever here; they have put themselves in a win win situation. If the submarine is not lifted this year due to weather of failure of the project they can proclaim that if the Russian divers had not been forced out of the sat team and replaced by Dutch it would have been successful. On the other hand if there is a successful conclusion to the project and she is brought to the surface they can proclaim there efforts were the reason for success. You must remember DSND have taken a contract which forbids them to make any self promotional claims so we in theory can not turn round and denounce either the Dutch or the Russians claims. The Dutch in their effort to convince us that their divers are up to the standards required for the job, are claiming that there divers are the best in the world and one particular diver they claim is the" best burner in the world". What they fail to understand is we do not object to the divers on their abilities in the water, its the fact that it will be their first time in saturation and this not the job for your first sat, its very high profile and high pressure. The other problem is the other divers have to have confidence in there abilities, if they get in to trouble they need to know that their dive partners will be able to help. Claiming you divers are the best and will show us how it is done is either a brave or stupid claim, ill go for the latter.

The weather is still not good enough for a chopper, the oncoming crew are being put up in a hotel in Murmansk until the weather is good enough for the choppers to fly. While onboard we have the off going crew are like bears with soar heads wanting off, claiming the relief's will be to drunk to turn up if they are left to long in a hotel. We also have a over manning problem now, because the decision has been made to decompress the Russians that will put their presence surplus to requirements. There are about 20 Russians who will not have to much to do, I expect they will down man, I do think they like it on here the food is far better than they are used to in the navy they have commented to me on more than one occasion. If they do go I will miss them I like to think of them as my friends now, we will still require the submarine engineers Rubin for their expertise on the Kursk. There is a 2100hr tea ritual that has seems to have established itself with the Admiral at this time in the evening, he will sit around a table with tree or four of his officers in the mess they have tea and a chat. I was invited to night to have a chat with the Admiral with the help of the interpreter we conversed I asked him how he felt about the decision to decompress the Russian team he had resided himself to the fact it was going to happen whether he liked it or not. We chatted and I discovered he was an navy champion swimmer I knew he was fit I see him most days in the gym working out, he is a very interesting man I would really like to get to know them better. I expect his team will be left to monitoring duties, they have video cameras in there offices and can watch exactly what we are doing 24 hours a day, make sure we not stealing any state secrets.

I had a conversation with the ROV(remote operated vehicle its a machine with cameras and thrusters and are used for observation) he informed me of a macabre find at the beginning of the contract, I was blissfully unaware of any finds of human remains, but he disclosed to me within the first couple of days of the job a boot was found with the remains of the foot inside, it was decided that this was not to be made known to the crew for fear of depressing people so soon into the contract, and thank god to date we have not had any other finds of that sort. Later when we are working inside the submarine we may have to deal with such finds.

23ʳᵈ AUGUST

Three o'clock in the morning - shift over (put in a bit of overtime today) Had a full day of diving, working on cleaning out 4:1, 4:2, 4:3, and 4:5. By tomorrow we'll have only Compartment III to cut. During the night they are going to concentrate on getting outer hull segments off on III - the port and starboard sides. If we get them off, we'll be cooking on gas, but it's a lot of work.

Andre. the chief Russian diver, gave me a couple of presents for my kids today knowing I was due to go home for 10 days, it was two of those little Russian dolls the one's that fit inside each other, I now know why he was so interested in the gender of my kids and their ages. I was totally caught of guard by this generous gesture, I felt a bit embarrassed I did not know what to say

The chopper was postponed again the guys are really impatient to get off but the weather was too rough, It might come tomorrow. There are rumours that the press visit may happen at the same time, I can't imagine what it will look like when they get of the helicopter and witness a mad rush from the off going crew to get on.

The Dutch are still trying to get their diver into "sat", I think some of the Russians still think it will not happen and someone from on high will step in and stop it at the last moment.

We had another visit to-day from some Russian visitor we get quite a few visits mainly to see the Russian team onboard they land and take of again in their military choppers the only time we see them is at meal time when the visits seem to coincide with, which begs the question are we feeding the Russian fleet. But to-days visitor was on a different mission he asked to speak to Sean my boss. It turned out that he was a naval officer and was granted permission to visit us because as he explained to Sean his son was one of the poor souls in the Kursk he thanked us for the work we were doing to bring his son home. He also asked if it was possible for us to retrieve a small section of the forward compartment for him to keep, this is were his son would have been at the time of the tragedy. We did manage to find some of the steel from that area and gave it to him he was very grateful. After he had gone Sean decided we could do better then that, we found another piece and asked Doug our dive tech if he could make it in to some kind of presentation for the officer. Doug did a fantastic job he polished up the steel and made a small brass submarine which fitted in the centre all placed in a presentation box. We asked the Russians if they could arrange for him to re-visit the vessel. The navel officer did re-visit the Mayo Sean's intention was this to be a low key affair just himself and the officer. Unfortunately the Russian did not, and made it a big presentation with high ranking officers in attendance. Sean was embarrassed for the man, he was very moved and close to tears this was a very private matter he was *obviously still grieving. There are some things and experiences that make you stop and reasses your life that was one.*

24th AUGUST

We had more problems with the weather yesterday we did not manage to get in the water until 2200hrs, we completed 4:5 and we another four ready for the holes to be cut. We also have the starboard side of compartment III cleared and ready for the hole to be cut, the port side still has a lot to do. We had a little altercation in sat control with the Admiral, as mentioned earlier the last Russian team have started decompressing. Before you can start this operation an 8 hour hold is enforced before the decompression can start. After the 8 hour hold was up the divers were moved into the decompression chamber, sat control was invaded by the Admiral and his entourage demanding what is going on. When it was explained to him what was going on he demanded they stopped what they were doing. This was confusing to all involved because they have known for days the decompression was going to happen. To me it looks like posturing and not losing face, whether it was for the benefit of Smit I don't know but it's a very strange set of affairs. Wally is the middle man in all this, Smit will not talk directly to the Admiral and visa versa Wally has been designated messenger man. Well end result is still the same they are continuing decompressing. There are a lot of unhappy Russians onboard now may be the Admiral had not informed his team what was occurring. The Dutch divers are here now and are to go into sat soon; they have nominated their superstar burner to go in first. I wonder if he knows how much he has been talked up by his superiors in Smit "the best burner in the world" was their claim about him. You can imagine our divers are waiting for him to fail which is not fair on him, but he now unwittingly finds himself in this position. Some of the Russian divers had to go off to-day to make way for the oncoming Dutch, they were not to happy about that. The weather is steadily getting worse it will only take a couple of days to jeopardise the project so close and yet so far. We have started a sweepstake for the nearest time for the last hole to be completed, the most favourite dates seem to be 28th to the 1st I reckon a little later ill wait a little longer before placing my money.

25th AUGUST

More weather problems we didn't manage to get in the water until 1700hrs we got straight into burning we can not afford to let up now. We could not overboard the hole cutter because the weather was to bad and we can't afford to damage that as it goes over we will be up shit creek without a paddle. I had to run the new team which included the Dutchman with the best burning credentials in the world. After observing him in action I don't have any problems with his in water abilities, but I didn't think I would. He is no better or worse than the guys in the team already. The weather is still not abating we need to get the cutter over the side soon to get these holes cut.

There's a rumour going round now which was brought on by the oncoming crew that the hole we have been cutting are the wrong size the dimensions sent were the wrong ones and there will not be enough clearance for the grippers to fit into. To be honest I don't give it much credence, somebody stirring it for god knows what reason because if it is true we may as well pack our bags and go home. We will carry on regardless we intend to finish the holes by Wednesday a lot will depend how we get on with compartment III. It was funny to-day not having the Russian team no interpreter to talk to, back to normal for me, direct communication. Its been a while since I've not had to go through an interpreter to do anything. It was a bit different, a lot less stressful, I can tell you.

The press were supposed to come on today but apparently it's been put off until tomorrow. I think that's the next day the weather will be good enough to take a helicopter. Better shave tonight just in case I get myself on the telly (Hollywood may beckon). Yesterday one of the Russian supervisors took me to one side and tried to give me a half a bottle of vodka, for myself and one of the other supervisors. He thought he was doing us a big favour; I tried to tell him if I got caught with alcohol I would be fired. I think the Russians have been in possession of vodka from day one, with all the helicopters coming and going they have been replenishing at will. It was still nice of them to offer because it means they have accepted me into their confidence.

26th AUGUST

To-day was the day the media turned up in force; they were all over the place with the cameras. There was to be a live link from dive control to some news channel in America. Brian (basher) Bates who had just arrived on the project happened to be on the panel when the door to dive control flung open and in rushed journalists and cameramen from CBS straight up to basher and started filming and questioning live on air, my big moment stolen from me Ill never make Hollywood now. I did ask for my picture to be taken I think they did just to keep me happy, so it was basher the star to-day. Later a very old gentleman came into dive control he was Russian and had a very large camera hanging around his neck. With the help of the interpreter he asked if he could take some photo's, he explained he was the official photographer for the highest of ranks in the Russian government and had photographed all the presidents for the last 50 years. He took his photo's was very particular with how we should stand and where, it was amazing to think I had my photograph taken by someone who took Brezhnev's.

Work wise we've had a very good day. At this point in time we've got 22 coupons completed and four to go. We still hope to do this by Wednesday. We're getting there. We've opened Compartment III on the starboard side now and hopefully by tomorrow we should have most of that out, and maybe even marked up for the hole. So we're going at it like trains. As long as the weather holds I think we'll have this done before we go off on Wednesday.

Most of the day's been taken up with the media etc, but we still managed to get some good work done. The sweepstake's going strong now for the finishing of the holes, some of our more optimistic people have lost already, but there is a lot of money riding on the 28th I still think it will be later.

27th AUGUST

Two thirty in the morning, quite a busy day. We've opened up compartments III either side of the conning tower we have actually cut 3:1 this leaves us with three to do. Hopefully when I come on shift there will be another two ready for the holes to be cut. We are at crisis stage now the oxygen for the burning is getting low it will be touch and go whether we will be able to complete the clearance area for the final hole. There is more oxygen on the barge but it would mean a delay, they will not go for that and carry on setting up for the barge to cut of the front section, which means we would not finish the holes before the barge sets up. We've actually cut 3:1 which leaves three to do. We completed the survey on the cut line of Compartment I and it's definitely cut all the way down to the sea bed. We are trying to establish if we can route the cutting wire through the submarine at seabed level. It would save time. The wire would snag on all the debris if we have to work it down the proposed cut line from the top of the submarine. The cut line's only half a metre from the first silo on the starboard and it's open. One of the divers had a look in there yesterday. You can see the granite missile popping out, or hanging out, so they are still umming and erring about whether the vibration of the cutting could do anything to this missile. I don't expect so, but you have to consider these things.

The sweepstake's looking good for the people on Tuesday early hours, that's where my money is so I stand a chance of winning a few bob. I don't see much of the Russians these days. They seem to keep themselves to themselves I think they had a party next door in the Admiral's cabin last night. They were laughing away until about two in the morning having some fun, this did not go down to well with Fitz next door who had to get up and tell them to keep the noise down. I do not think the Admiral is used to people telling him what to do, but they did turn it down.

28th AUGUST

Two o'clock in the morning. As I finished shift at 12 o'clock we'd cut 25 holes. They're just cutting the last one. So I reckon about 5 o'clock in the morning the last hole will be out. That will make Smit happy; another stage payment of 25% of the project has to be paid which will be a tidy sum. The barge has sailed from Kirkeness we were hoping it wouldn't, we could then sail in and do the crew change in port. Looks like that will not happen now because we have to be here when she arrives and assist as necessary. It will have to be a chopper crew change through Murmansk and the long bus journey to Kirkeness. There will be a lot of people going off on this crew change which will mean lot of delays if the other lads experience's are anything to go by.

We've trimmed the mast, again as requested by the engineers now its ready to be lifted, we are concentrating on the proposed cut line for the barge, our divers will have to thread the cutting wire through the submarine if they go for the site we have proposed. We have been seen on TV apparently, one of the lads phoned home and his wife said we were on the television stardom at last. I have been up in the offices of the Russians to-day just nattering about everything and nothing; I will miss them when they go. I'm just looking forward to going home right now. Got a funny feeling there's going to be some delays, so I'm not expecting to reach home for a couple of days.

29_{th} AUGUST

Two o'clock in the morning and just finished shift. I'm preparing to go home for two weeks I'm looking forward to that. We finished the last coupon, took it out about one o'clock. They're all out now and we've just been trimming up for the rest of the day. NCA have caught the big PR teams of Smit and Mammoet napping they managed to announce first on the Internet that they have completed the holes, stealing their thunder it was also accompanied with some footage of the cutter in action an interview with their company chairman, they must have pre planned this. I say well done, of course our company are not allowed to acknowledged the fact we are involved.

The barge is on its way and due tomorrow evening, we're running out of oxygen so I think the cutting will stop fairly soon. That's about it for the rest of the day and hopefully I'll be gone by the time it arrives. All the worlds press should be at Murmansk we are led to believe, so that should be interesting. I am being told by sat control that a virus has been recorded in the chambers, this is a disaster once you get a virus in the saturation chambers it will be in there for along time some people are susceptible to catching bugs but under pressure they can manifest themselves in some horrible ways. I am sure it will still be a problem when I get back. There will have to be a very strict cleaning regime adopted until it's eradicated.

The helicopter has arrived and its time to go, it's a Russian helicopter which is not like our helicopters these are used for air sea rescue. The pilots are reported to be the best in the navy when I had been pre warned by my mates that the standards are not quite the same as what we are used to. As I boarded I remember seeing the wire reinforcing showing through the tyres of the helicopter. One story going about is that on one flight the side door fell of, the helicopter just landed picked it up and carried on as if nothing had happened. The inside was very cramped with not much head room the bulk of the space was taken up by the rotor engine, we threw in our bags and jumped in, found our very uncomfortable seats the noise was so loud we could not communicate we got a thumbs up and we took off. I was sitting opposite the side door and the story of one falling off was in the fore front of my mind, I double checked my seat belt and kept my fingers crossed. Soon after take off the load master opened the side door anyway and most of the flight was very loud noise but beautiful scenery below I really enjoyed the flight. We landed in what I think was a military airport we disembarked in a corner out of site of the main terminal in what looked like a helicopters grave yard, there were bits of helicopters all over the place not one complete one amongst them. It looked like mechanics were cannibalising parts to repair the least broken ones. We were then transported to the terminal in a little mini bus and were escorted through customs. Our company in its wisdom had given us paperwork in the event of problems with the officialdom of Russia, stating that we were members of the Kursk salvage team and are working with the Russian Federal Navy. Believing this information will glide us through any problems we may encounter and possibly assist us in getting preferential treatment was short lived when presented to the first custom official who looked at it and shrugged, our company in their wisdom had written it in English which of course no one could read it. We passed though customs I had a little scare because I had in my baggage the bottle of Diver Vodka that Andre had given me and this was supposed to be a dry project no alcohol on board , but after explaining who gave me it they let me through. It was a very big airport but not many people about we seem to have the place to ourselves. We were escorted to a large bus which was going to take us across the tundra to Kirkeness in Northern Norway. One of the NCR cutting operators was Russian and was used as an unofficial interpreter on the journey; he asked if we wanted to go to the local supermarket in Murmansk to by souvenirs or beer for the journey. After discussions with the driver he took us to the local shopping centre, we went inside this crumbling building where there were a few Kiosks selling bits and pieces , we found a shop that sold beer and vodka where a substantial amount was bought. Out side there was a small market were people were selling things from the back of vans laid out on the floor it looked like most of the local trade was conducted here. We set of for kirkeness as we left we were flagged down by the police if it wasn't for the fact they were going to arrest the driver it would have been funny. We were going about five miles per hour when this policeman walked out in front of the bus and pointed what looked like a gun at the bus , the driver stopped and was asked to get out. At this point our interpreter told us they were going to arrest the driver unless he pays a fine, apparently we were speeding and it was a radar speed gun they pointed at us. He explained it is the kick back the police expect from any driver who drives through their territory it was only a few quid put it left a sour taste in my mouth. When we eventually got going on our journey leaving Murmansk behind us over a very rickety bridge, the scenery soon turned to the tundra wide open space of nothing we passed some military barracks and warned not to take photo's, tanks and armoured vehicles all over the place. We came across our first check point in the middle of nowhere this poor soldier was in this hut with no other signs of civilisation for miles around, he stopped the bus and asked to see our passports as he passed through the bus it was obvious he was checking visa's. Fitz and myself did not have visa's because we came into Russia via the Mayo, sailing in we did not have any paperwork. When he looked at my passport he said something which to me sounded like you are a spy I will take you outside and shoot you, he also said something similar to Fitz and left the coach with our passports. The bus being half pissed by now concluded with my thoughts and said there farewells to us , but luck was with us and the guard came back on the coach gave us back our passports then preceded to try and sell trinkets he had made to us all. Walking up and down the bus with a replica of a guard's tower made out what looked like barb wire with his Kalashnikov slung over his shoulder pressure salesman or what. When he decided that there were no art novo lovers onboard he lifted his gate and let us pass. We had the famous cafe to visit next I won't tell you why it but it to do with the artistic creation of its content and the dexterity of the last visitor all I can say the oncoming crew said if you stop at the cafe you must go look in the toilet on the opposite side of the road it was of a thunder box type creation. We did stop, visited the now famous toilet bought some more beer and some Russian delicacies and continued on our way. Another landmark we had to look out for was Nickel city; this was a nickel producing factory in the middle of the tundra which a small town had grown up on the upwind side of the factory. It was explained to me you will Know you are approaching Nickel city much earlier than the sight of buildings. The wind blows predominately one way, eastward I think the smoke from the factory has killed the vegetation on the eastward side of the factory for many miles, as we approached we could see the ground scorched and black with no sign of life for mile after mile. When we came upon the factory it looked to me like the most desolate place to live on this earth, soon as you get to the westward side of the factory the vegetation lives once again, those poor inhabitants have to breath the same pollution. After a few more remote check points we arrive at the border control we have been pre warned about a possible delay of five hours. We line up to for the first baggage search we were also warned that if any souvenirs from the kursk were found not only would they be confiscated possible arrest and loss of job would be the outcome. We were very lucky it took only about one hour and we were back in the bus stopped at the last check point offered one more chance to buy a replica tower made from barb wire, and we were into Norway. We spent the night in a hotel in Norway there were a couple of hotels in Kirkeness we had a nice one close to the museum. After I had checked into the hotel we had a bit of time to kill the flight home was not until the next day. The Kirkeness museum is an amazing place; it tells how kirkeness was the most bombed place during the Second World War. It was constantly fought over by the Russians and the Germans its coast line overlooks the sea that the Atlantic convoys passed through to re-supply Russia during the war. Who ever held Kirkeness controlled the shipping lanes. There were several concentration camps there as well one camp housed nothing but teachers and they were forced to build a road ,it is known as teachers road to this day. A very interesting museum if you ever get the chance it worth a visit. Later that evening we met in the bar and had a few drinks, we were aware of the journalist about and what happened to the last crew who came trough here so we kept to ourselves. The next day we caught our flight and made our separate ways home, it was a very long journey but worth it to get back home to normality.

During the time I was at home my mind kept returning to the Kursk project how was the cutting of the front section coming along, I was listening out on the TV and radio for any news reports. I decided to buy some presents for the Russians who showed me kindness, I took my family on a visit to Scarborough and found a T shirt shop selling shirts with large British bulldogs on wearing union jacks I bought 20 of them for the Russians, weather they would wear them on this job I doubt, I also visited a watch shop in Ripon(North Yorkshire) and spoke to the manageress I wanted to buy the Russian dive supervisors a G shock diving watch, they did admire my one I have always worn one think they are good. I explained what I was doing and that I wanted to buy 5 watches could she do me a deal. She was very nice and gave me a good discount on four and a free one, so if you ever read this I thank you again. I bought a book on the history of Britain for Alex the interpreter. I also bought about ten

Yorkshire rose pin badges, so I could pass the on the great county of Yorkshire to the Russians. As with all the time at home it passes very quickly and before you know it you get the telephone to go back to work. This time it was a little different because in this case I wanted to go back and finish this job.

10th SEPTEMBER

I started my long journey back to the Mayo I caught my early morning taxi to Leeds, flight to Paris where I met up with Glen a sat tech and we travelled together to Oslo, where we met a few more of the crew. We managed to get a beer there before the flight to Kirkeness. We were met at the airport in Kirkeness with a bus to take us to the town, we were to stay here for the evening and set of for Murmansk in the morning. The Hotel was not as good as the one we stayed in on the way home, they tell us all the rooms in the other hotels were fully booked. It is more likely a better deal here for the company. I went out for a walk there are still some media people around, I wandered down to the docks and I discovered the Giant 4 barge there. This is the barge which will be lifting the Kursk in the not to distant future. There were a police guard at the bottom of the gang plank, which was keeping a small posse of reporters at bay. The barge is very big as you would expect, the jacking equipment are lined up on the deck like a Manhattan sky line. They are all covered with tarpaulins to keep the photographers at arms length .She looked deserted I spoke to the guard on the vessel and he told me that there was only a couple onboard. As you may have detected I am not a big fan of Smit but you have to take your hat of to the engineering involved in converting this barge to lift the submarine, the hole alignment has to be spot on for this to work. The Mammoet lifting jacks are a proven method of lifting just are being used in a different environment. I am impressed with the barge it does fill me with confidence that it will happen. After a quick walk around the town, I came across the lads in a pub drinking like there is no tomorrow so I had to assist. I stumbled into bed at dark o clock.

11th SEPTEMBER

Before you know it the early call has arrived and its time for breakfast then the now infamous bus journey to Murmansk I am not looking forward to that. Everyone is present so we board the bus I suppose with a bit more anticipation this time, we will be hopefully lifting the Kursk this trip. We stop at customs on the Norwegian side of the border and we go through the first of many passport controls. The custom officials knew who we were and wished us luck with the Lift. We met the stony faces of the Russian custom officers and after the obligatory wait for god knows what reason we are sent on our way. After the initial burst of enthusiasm we settle down and try and catch some sleep. After a while I was expecting to see Nickel city but when it did not appear I asked the driver where it was , through hand gestures, nods and finger pointing I discovered that we have bypassed the town. I am led to believe that the Russians were not impressed with our comments of the city and approved a different route to Murmansk this time. We pass through he same check points as before I wonder how long these poor guards are posted in the middle of nowhere being an ex serviceman I can empathise with them. We re-visit our famous cafe and toilet which to our relief has been cleaned since we last visited. We have a beer and a sandwich and climb wearily back into the bus for the last leg of the journey to Murmansk. We arrive early evening in Murmansk and are dropped of at our hotel, the plan is to stay the evening here and we will be picked up in the morning and taken to the airport for the helicopter flight to the vessel. As usual in these situations we check in drop of our bags in the room and congregate in the bar for drinks. When I arrived in the hotel bar I ordered three beers and as I took my first quaff right in front of me mounted up high was the bar television and as I drank I saw the first plane hit the twin towers, at first I thought it was a film and as I watched I realised something was not right I asked the bartender to turn up the volume it was CNN and they were explaining it was live coverage of what was happening in New York. I could not take it in what was going on, as we discussed what we saw the 2ⁿᵈ plane crashed into the twin towers. It was totally disbelieving what I was seeing. I returned to my room and turned on the television and watched all night waiting for someone to come on and say it was all some sick hoax like the war of the world's hoax that happened in America 20 years before. Un- fortunately it was not to be and many thousands of poor souls were lost that day, those few hours alone in a hotel in Russia watching that devastation happening in America will stay with me for the rest of my life.

12ᵗʰSEPTEMBER

We received our early morning call, staggered down stairs for breakfast. It was a very unusual breakfast not what we were used to it reminded me of when we used to queue up for lunch at school with the dinner ladies dishing out the food, and all this was accompanied by a man in the corner playing an accordion. I do not know what that was about but he was playing for all he was worth, not actually foot tapping music for that time in the morning very surreal. The main topic of conversation as you would expect was the twin towers, it still hasn't sunk in yet it just doesn't seem possible that something like that could happen. After breakfast we gather in the foyer after a quick roll call we board the bus. This is the time we learn of any antics that has gone on during the night by our younger and more exuberant colleagues. The hotel had its quota of ladies of the night and a couple of our lads the worst for wear went of with two ladies, we had been forewarned of the dangers of wandering of from the hotel. These two ended up in a block of flats somewhere in the city not knowing were they were or how to get back to the hotel. They were lucky a good Samaritan came to their rescue, got them a taxi and pointed them in the right direction. They arrived in time to catch the bus, if not a few dollars light but memories in the bank. Our journey to the airport was uneventful when we arrived it was as before no one around this massive car park and we were the only vehicle there. We had a long wait for the helicopter flight they fed us and looked after us well, but it was how I imagined Russia to be everything grey, large buildings unsmiling faces. We passed through immigration with no problem and boarded our flight it was much the same as when we came of two weeks earlier very noisy but lovely scenery. We landed ok, as I said before they are very good pilots and it was a smooth landing as we disembark we have just enough time to say hello and goodbye to the off going crew as we pass one another.

When we left two weeks prior we had just finished cutting the holes and the barge ATM Carrier was due on site that night. What's happened since then is that the barge set up, though they've had their fare share of problems. The two massive suction anchors were installed this is a tried and tested method anchorage system for moorings each anchor consisted of a large diameter steel tube open at the bottom a suction pump mounted on the top when the tube is sat on the sea-bed and a seal is formed the suction pump is activated which reduces the pressure internally causing a vacuum, this vacuum causes the tubes to be sucked down into the sea bed its a very smooth operation , to retract the anchors air is pumped into the void therefore over pressurising the anchors which forces the anchors out of the sea-bed very simple but effective. The suction anchors were placed either side of the submarine adjacent to the proposed cut line. There was a hydraulic system mounted on the suction anchors and the abrasive sawing cable was attached and laid across the submarine. As I mentioned earlier this method of cutting a section from a vessel in not knew the difference this time is where as the usual method is to run the abrasive wire under the vessel and cut upwards the motion of the salvage vessel on the sea is used to saw the section off, the natural rocking of the vessel is enough to move the wire back and forth sawing through the stricken vessel on the sea floor. We had to saw downward because the engineers were worried if we cut upwards the motion of the sawing could dislodge the submarine from its settled down position i.e. it could roll over on its side and may even break up, so the downward method was deemed less likely. This process was going to be a diver less operation because of the unaccounted torpedo's in the front section and the possibility of the vibration setting of a missile it was deemed to be to dangerous for the diver to be there. The Mayo was to be sitting off from the site in a clear area monitoring radiation levels, at certain intervals the cutting would cease and the Mayo would move in and the ROV would go in and check the progress of the cutting, because the cutting barge's only means of communication with the saw wire were the gauge's top side indicating the amount of tension required to move the wire back and forth with the increasing tonnage to move the wire indicating the wire cutting in to the submarines steel hulls, the theory being when the pressure drops of this would indicate the wire had cut through both hulls and severed the front section off, an angle was put on the cut so when the submarine is lifted it will not catch the section to be left on the bottom. There are rumours that the front section will be left on the bottom because the Russians do not want it up because of the evidence that would destroy their theory of a collision with an American submarine. This rumour was squashed when it was announced that they will recover the front section next summer. Well I have just explained the theory of Smit's system for removing the front section now I will tell you what happened, as I was on leave when the cutting took place I can only relay what my fellow workmate told me for this to happen. I mentioned earlier that we surveyed the cut line with divers who indicated that there was a natural crack from the top to the bottom which could accommodate the cutting wire leaving only the section buried to be cut this was deemed unusable by the powers that be, and a knew cut line was ordered just in front of the conning tower. From the very start the cutting was not as we would have liked it was jamming up to much and before long the divers were called upon to go into the submarine and free up the wire, on a couple of occasions the wire snapped and the divers had to enter the submarine again to change out the cutting wire and then thread the wire back down through the cut line or it would mean restarting the cut which was not what they wanted to do. Eventually the wire made its slow progress through the steel hulls of the submarine until eventually the pressure top side dropped of and Smitt claimed the section was severed. The divers were asked to go in and confirm this; because the front section was partially buried the divers could not see the cutting wire and could not confirm or deny that the section was fully severed. This caused problems because the front section being fully severed was critical to the lift the Russians were not convinced that it was and wanted more proof. The only proof offered was the pressure gauge read outs from the tensioners for the saw wire, this did not convince Ruben the design engineers there conclusion was that the wire could have broke which it had in the past this would also give a pressure drop off. We had a Mexican stand of Ruben saying it's not cut Smitt telling them it was. Ruben wanted to do another cut Smit said no it would take to long which might delay the lift until next year a lot was at stake,

While all this was going on I have been playing father Christmas I've just been passing out a my presents I brought back for the Russians and it makes me feel good because they are chuffed with them. I gave out the T shirts to the Russian divers they did look a bit bewildered with the British bulldog wearing a union jack shirt but they excepted them with good grace I did ask them to wear them instead of their uniforms but some how I don't think they will. I gave out the watches to the supervisors and the look on their faces was worth it Andrei insisted that I take his watch in return Its a submariners watch with a picture of a Russian sub on it. I gave the Admiral a watch too and came to me later *with a box of chocolates as a thank you. I had a couple of presents for Andrei's children in return for the Russian dolls for my kids I got them to pick what presents to get for Andrei's children. Alex the interpreter received a book about England and its history which he was happy about. I got calculators for the Rubens engineers I was working with, I also had bought some Yorkshire rose pins and I gave one to Sergei who was the chief engineer of the Kursk he was the back to back for the chief engineer who perished, he is a very nice man and said he would always wear the pin. Well all my presents are given out now and I feel good about it and I hope it has cemented our friendship a little more. When I left for leave I mentioned there was a case of infection in the sat system, this can be a very big problem if it is not caught and dealt with straight away, unfortunately the Smit divers infection was so bad he had to be decompressed the infection spread to others who were decompressed as well to cure it the infected chamber had to be surfaced and a thoroughly disinfected that seemed to do the trick, it doesn't take much for bugs to run wild in sat its a perfect culturing ground for them. With the last two infected personnel decompressing we think we have cleared it. With the front section cut of now we are back at work we have to install the gripper guide cones and clear the underside of the holes for the lifting anchors to be installed. When we cleared section three and removed the coupons 3:1 which is port side forward the debris there was unbelievable, this demonstrated the force of the blast to me all the forward machinery had been compressed and forced back when the coupon was removed we could see the crumpled periscope and a mass of machinery which filled the void to the top of the sub there was no clearance from the hole we had cut downwards. This will give us a headache trying and get the clearance required for the lifting anchors. The new estimated date for the lift is 20th/21st/ or 22nd it could be all over by the end of the month we will need plenty of luck for that to happen.*

13th SEPTEMBER

The saga of the front section is still continuing Smit are insisting it is severed the Russian Federation Navy also agree its been severed but Rubens designers on the vessel and in St Petersburg do not agree they still want more proof insisting it could be a snapped wire which has given the pressure drop on the gauges. After another inspection of the cut area we are no nearer convincing them, the cut line is totally obscured now, debris has fallen back on itself and the line can not be distinguished now. Smitt have offered a compromise, to appease the engineers will leave the suction anchors in position and drop the surfaces hoses to the sea bed, if the submarine's front section is not fully cut they will be able to bring back the barge reconnect the hoses and finish the cut if this satisfies Ruben the ATM Carrier cutting barge could weigh anchor and head to port mission accomplished . The reality is as soon as that barge leaves it will not come back, it would a nightmare of a job to try and reconnect the barge back up to the cutting wire and continue cutting. Having talked to the Smit salvage experts onboard they really believe the main pressure hull is cut through they had readings of 40ton pressure on there gauges when sawing and it dropped of to 10ton that convinced them the main hull is cut, but they are not so sure about the outer hull, that is only 10mm thick steel and 150mm of sonar rubber it would break of when lifted it may tear a little but will not be a problem. We will have to wait and see if the engineers in St Petersburg will be satisfied with the compromise offered, we are wasting valuable time while this decision is being made.

14th SEPTEMBER

Seven o'clock in the evening. We still are awaiting a decision on whether we have to cut the front section some more. It has been reported on the internet that we have completed the cut, I do not know where there information comes from, we are still waiting officially from St Petersburg that they except Smit's conclusion that its cut and the compromise of dropping the hoses is excepted. As I said before I believe the compromise is just a ploy to placate Rubens. If we pick the submarine up there is no way we will put it back down unless it breaks up then it will be game over anyway. I and many others thought we'd get an answer today, tomorrow is the weekend so whether we'll get anything then we don't know. We are just continuing chopping away around the access holes to get these gripper guides in. About two o'clock to half past, the weather picked up and because we're working in the anchor pattern off the ATM Carrier we are far more susceptible to weather, we had to pull off. We've been pulled off hours now waiting for the weather to drop so we can go back in.

I don't know where the media get their dates from, I suspect from the internet. They are now predicting that we are going to pick it up on the 25th, which is ten days away. I can't see that. Even if the barge has gone tomorrow, and we've been given full rein to get in there, I still don't think we'll get there by the 25th. The Giant 4 lift barge still has got to sail out, set up, and then we've got to connect up her lifting equipment to the "Kursk". We calculated that's going to take five or six days to do that. If we get done by the end of the month we'll be doing well.

We have experienced some problems with the divers radiation monitors, we have had readings up to 900 and the maximum is 1000 the experts believe it's a duff batch as we have not recorded any high readings to date. Erring on the side of safety we have implemented more stringent safety regimes, we are convinced its faulty meters. We had one of the top navel men on board today having a look around - also some news people following in his wake asking all sorts of questions and filming anything that moves.

15th SEPTEMBER

Eight o'clock at night just finished shift. The big thing today was the departure of the barge this morning. It picked its anchor after dropping the suction hoses on the seabed, as we anticipated Smit won the day with Rubin as we thought they would. We took the opportunity to take on fuel water and food, so now we're stocked up to the gunwales, enough to finish the job the end is in sight now.

We're getting into burning and cutting and installing guide clamps now and we're getting the subfucker ready. The subfucker is like a big battering ram phallic in shape very long and weighs about 5 ton it is designed to fit snugly into the hole we have cut it has an mark on the side to indicate if we can get the subfucker to that mark then the grippers will fit(for obvious reasons we nicknamed her subfucker) there is also an hydraulic ram on the side which is designed to clear any obstructions in the areas where the lifting plates will eventually sit when activated from the surface. We intend to use it as a battering ram for now until we start to get the penetration required. It should be up and running by the time I come on shift tomorrow the Dutch designer is onboard to supervise the use of his creation, with a bit of luck it should work fine. We are looking at the 23rd of September as our best guess for the lift now it's not unusual in this part of the world for the winter weather to close in about now. The race is on to beat the weather the Russian divers are saying it could change in a very short time here, and they should know this is there work area.

We had a chopper in today to change out some of the Ruben's submarine engineers, the internal and equipment specialists are being changed out for the pressure hull designers its there hull that will take the weight of the submarine when we eventually lift her. Vladimir and Vassily are back, Vassily has brought the stamps he promised for my daughter and they are very special I was expecting a few stamps from the post office but these were like special sets in cellophane packets and looked quite expensive I asked Alexander the interpreter to tell Vassily that I can not take them without paying for them, Alexander said he would not translate that for it would embarrass him and it would be rude for me to offer money. I did not know what to do I thanked him profusely. I am glad these two are back I had gained a bit of a rapport with them and I think we had started to appreciate each others humour.

16th SEPTEMBER

Its eight o'clock in the evening - just finished shift. Today we continued cleaning out Compartment IV, externally and internally. We completed all of the holes in that Compartment by mid-day. It's been inspected and accepted by Rubin and Smit we have permission to start to install the gripper guides inn this compartment we started earlier installing them in compartment V earlier. We've installed the first guide on 4:2. we will be continue through the night to install all the gripper guides in Compartment IV. We had a good look in Compartment III which we anticipate will be the worst area, we think we will have no problem with 3:1, 3:2 is really going to be the hardest one, as I said before the explosion in the forward Compartment has pushed the front two Compartments back into Compartment III and beyond. To clear out that section for the grippers the divers will have to burn from the inside of the submarine which will mean entering the holes we have cut to clear the internal debris. In this case it's the periscope which is a mangled mess in there, this was risked assess as to dangerous and the Russian did not want us to enter the submarine an the beginning of the contract but now it's the only alternative we have to clear this section. During the burning operations one of the divers suffered a blow back Its a build up of combustible o2 forming a pocket of gas then ignites causing an explosion depending on the size of the gas pocket depicts the size and ferocity of the explosion which can and have been in the past proved fatal. This time it was enough to crack the divers face plate of his helmet which must have been a fair old bang. He was unhurt just a bit of shock we recovered him with no further incident, Just a change of hat was required.

I've just been chewing the fat with the Russians Navy dive team, I think they are getting just a bit bored now. Their main task now is to constantly watch the monitors in their office which relays the diver's hat mounted cameras pictures to them. This they perform diligently 24/7 they have at least two people watching at all times, keeping an eye on us to see if we do not stray into areas we shouldn't. They still have input into the recovery but we are quickly approaching the technical part of the job, the connecting up and lifting with the Giant 4 barge. I think they will have more of a back seat position when this happens Rubens are very much in the decision making process their expertise is still fundamental to the success of the operation. Tomorrow is going to be more of the same, installing guides. Hopefully we can get Compartment III completed in the next couple of days, we have resorted to using the ships crane to remove the periscope from the void below hole 3:1 we hope brute strength will be enough tot pull the periscope out through the hole our options are very few. The captain of the ship is not happy with this method if we damage the crane beyond repair at sea then it jeopardises the project, he has restricted the amount of pull we can exert with the crane well within it's safe working capacity. Once this one is completed we will work towards the stern, we expect the guide installation easier as we progress towards the aft there is less hull damage the further we move from the explosion area. We are hoping to make up some time during this phase of the operation.

I've been told the Giant 4 barge is preliminarily booked to get here for the 23rd which is seven days away. That gives us a bit of time but also exerts a little more pressure on to us to be ready for her when she arrives.

17th SEPTEMBER

It's been a long day we've been installing gripper guides in Compartment IV. We've had quite a few problems installing them because some of the guides don't fit properly; either because of the welds on the submarine's frames where the guides fit clash with the guides or web plates in the way it has meant modifications as we go which is slowing thing down. The bolts used for installing the guides have to be torqued; some of the bolts have been shearing as we torque them. This is quite concerning to us these bolts will potentially experience eight ton of pressure I have been told, to seen them shear with just the torque pressure do not fill me with confidence. Smit has come up with an idea to lay a drag wire to the stern of the submarine which will be connected to a ocean going tug which will be positioned forward of the submarine. The theory which Smit tells me is a proven theory is for releasing the suction caused by the settlement of the submarine into the seabed. As the lift starts the tug will steam ahead dragging the wire under the submarine relieving the suction element from the equation. The theory seems good to me we come across this problem in the oilfield industry we normally over compensate the rigging for a sub-sea lift, not easily done for a lift this size. My thoughts are that the sonar rubber which encases the Kursk would stop the free run of the wire and it would bind up or dig into the rubber and cause problems rather then solve them. I can see how it would be a good idea under a steel hull but no the Kursks rubber coated one. Also what will happen when it hits the front section it will foul up with the debris and if that get entangled with the lift it could cause big problems. The wire is positioned now with marker buoys depicting the pick up points for the 2 tugs.

We completed Compartment V and have torqued up the guides now. We've got a further three guides to install in the front sections compartment 3 being the difficult one, not much room to manoeuvre the clamp or the diver to torque the bolts. Right now we're using the subfucker which is pushing some of the debris clear from Compartment III. There's a lot of debris in there to clear, because the weather's good they decided subfucking is the best option at this time .We are hoping this area will be cleared tomorrow it will be touch and go if it is. 3:2 is still causing us problems with the periscope, it is well jammed in there and the crane with the restriction imposed on us is not moving it, its made of very thick steel broccoing isn't an option either because we can't get access to it from above. I suppose we'll have to cut it up into small bits and pull them out with the crane. We'll find a way round it but it's not going to be easy.

18th SEPTEMBER

Much of the same to-day clearing out section 3:2 little by little, a person who shall remain nameless decided enough was enough, got the crane onto the periscope and gave it a pull of about 30 ton and it came out the captain was in bed so he never knew. Anyway it did the trick the periscope was out and with the access that gave the rest was soon cleared. This gives us a clear run at installing the guides in the front sections; hopefully we will make up some lost time the periscope caused us. The atmosphere on the vessel is getting more positive by the day, the end is in sight we just hope the weather holds for us. I have been told we must have a weather window of 5 days before we start to connect up the Giant 4 to the Kursk we could be in a situation where we are finished our bit and waiting for the 5 day weather window. It would be heart breaking now if we have everything ready for the lift and it gets called of because there is no weather window, doesn't bare thinking about.

19ᵗʰ SEPTEMBER

My daughter's birthday Cathryn is 11 to-day, it's another birthday I am not there for. I hope she forgives me. In my chosen work we tend to miss a lot of the family celebrations which shore based workers take for granted. All I can say in print is I am sorry I am not there; I love you and have a happy birthday.

We've now completed Compartment III with the guides Compartment IV is nearly completed. We've got a bit of welding repair to do but that won't take long. During the clearing phase for this compartment one of the submarines structural frames was accidentally cut into with a burning rod. This frame as it turned out was one of the chosen lifting frames which will take the weight of the submarine when we lift. The Ruben's designers were very concerned and were claiming this could be enough to cause the submarine to break up during the lift; this is just a 10cm burn into a massive structural frame. Well instead of going on about it just let us repair it, we welded the damaged area and ground it flush to reduce stress risers and eventually the Rubens designers reluctantly agreed that it was a good enough repair. I think this was more about us, we made a mistake and they wanted us to know they know. By the time I go on shift tomorrow I expect that entire Compartment to be completed. We'll be moving down to do Compartments V, VII and VIII. We're cracking on, they are talking about Sunday for the arrival of the Giant 4 on site and they want us to be ready to start connecting her up to the Kursk. We've received a ten day forecast of good weather, this is our five day weather window, we now have a deadline to work to and we need to pull all the stops out to be ready. It's a tight schedule we have I hope the forecast slips a day or two we may need the time.

Crew change today, this could be the last one on this job. We have a Smit diver in sat who has decided he doesn't like it, and wants to come out. He is claiming he has an ear infection and wants to come out on medical grounds. This is the same diver I had reservations about whether he really wanted to go in; I spoke to him before hand. I told him not to go into sat if he has any doubts as it will manifest into fear if he's not careful, I believe Smit who had just paid for him to do his saturation training course (£8,000) has put the pressure on him to go in. I think this is more about Smit not wanting to loose face after all the claims they had made about the ability of their divers, and how they should have been in sat from the beginning. Don't misunderstand me it's a brave thing to admit you do not want to go into sat or ask to be pulled from sat. It's not the nicest place to be when you don't want to be there. He has my respect for having the guts to come out with all the pressure there must be to stay in, I blame Smit for that. Chris the superstar burner, came out and his replacement came out as well the Dutch record for there divers in sat is not to good right now, and I don't think Smit like it. I think there's only one diver who's completed a trip so far, it doesn't make them look very good "sat" diving-wise. I'm not bragging or anything like that, divers are divers, and "sat" is not everybody's cup of tea, especially if you've been used to air diving for 20-odd years. You need a different mind set for sat diving, I do not want to sound like I am a I told you so person, in the beginning of this project when the Dutch divers were onboard we discussed the merit of putting divers into sat for their first time on such a high profile job, and we agreed it was not a good decision. Maybe that decision in hindsight should have prevailed.

Vladimir has returned to the ship for a visit, he was one of the Russian supervisors who was down manned when the Russian divers were pulled from sat. It was nice to meet him again Vladimir had visions of starting his own diving company when he left the navy and constantly asked questions about equipment and suppliers. I even introduced him to our technicians and he quizzed them for information and about repairing equipment.

20TH SEPTEMBER

It's eight o'clock in the evening. I've finished shift and today's been quite an eventful day. Compartment IV's completed, Compartment III is nearly completed and we've moved to Compartment V. At 11 o'clock this morning we had what we call in the trade a blow back with one of the divers working in Compartment V. Tom Ferguson and Steve Upwood were the divers and they were clearing the inside of the holes of any obstructions. In this compartment the holes are quite close together, if you can imagine a clock face the position of the holes were at about 11 and 1 o clock. Steve was burning in one and Tom was working in the other. When the blowback occurred (the build up of o2 suddenly exploding) Steve had his head in the hole he was working on and Tom just happened to be laying over the hole with is chest covering the hole. When the explosion erupted Steve suffered a ruptured ear drum and the shock wave passed through the hole Tom's body was covering which he took fully in the chest. We recovered the divers to the bell and recovered the bell; by the time they transferred through to the chambers we had a medically trained diver waiting to examine them. On examination he confirmed Steve had a perforated ear drum, this would end his diving on this project, and Tom had a bruised chest. On investigation into the incident we discovered that the insulation on the pressure hull was made of cork, we believe this acted like a sponge and absorbed the oxygen as Steve was working it eventually reached a point where when Steve made an arc with the burner it ignited the oxygen causing the explosion. As a result of this investigation we ceased all burning inside of the submarine, this will give us problems, how will we remove obstructions now? Smit were not happy with this decision they would be quite willing to let us carry on burning even after such an incident. This tells me the welfare of there divers is not as higher priority as it should be, the decision is made though we will not burn inside the submarine anymore. The lift contact zones on the underside of the holes will now have to be re-thought on how we will clear these areas without the burning gear. In these zones we are only aloud to leave stubs of 5mm or less our only other tool to achieve this would be grinders but that will slow us up big time. With the weather widow fast approaching this is the last thing we need right now. I suspect we'll get pressure from above to carry on burning, not from my own company, but from Smit. **(There is a post story to this incident. When the submarine was in dry dock and they were clearing out this section they discovered a large amount of explosives in this compartment which we believe the Russian federation Navy new about, it was a known storage area for this type of cargo)**

Besides that my shift was left to assess the equipment, check it all over, and make sure it was still serviceable. Then we just started to go back diving again our work was limited to external burning. Internally we used hydraulics etc. That's where we are right now. We've been working in Compartment VII, endeavouring to clear the lifting areas internally with disc grinders only, which are going to take a while.

21st SEPTEMBER

Today's been very slow, we've finished all the external clearance work in Compartment VII and we've still got the internals to do. The problems we had with Steve and Tom in holes 5:! And 5:2 *have been overcome with hydraulic grinders, a lot slower but they did the job. They've just passed the inspection and we can install the gripper guides. The design engineer has made a template the size of the gripper foot which we can offer up to the lifting point, then only clear what we have to in the contact zone. This will stop us clearing away obstructions that do not interfere with the jack foot area, it should be a big help. Tomorrow we should be compartment VII, I think three or four days until we are ready, I am guessing around about the 25th will be lift day if the weather holds fingers crossed.*

22nd SEPTEMBER

It's not been a very productive day today, now that we're not burning internally any more, using only the hydraulic grinders the progress has slowed right down. We still have another ten holes to complete, the subfucker's ram design is not working properly we are basically using it as a battering ram all the hydraulic design are not having much success. I think Smit are going to start loosing patient as the day goes on. The Giant 4 lift barge has set sail for the work site she will be with us soon, they are going to want to hook this submarine up a.s.a.p. and we are not going to be ready. The next few days should be interesting the pressure will be on, I have experienced pressure jobs in the oil industry before this is more intense. Vladimir and Vassily two of the Rubens engineers are leaving to-day and they have come round to say good bye I will miss them, Vladimir accompanied them the supervisor who is visiting us. A lot of photos were taken and promises of seeing each other again. The usual stuff one say's when bidding farewell I would really like to think we will see each other again. It's the beginning of the end for this project once key people start to leave. They wanted to stay to the end and watch the lift but with all the dignitaries coming onboard from Mammoet, Smit, Russian Navy & Ruben to witness the lifting phase beds are at a premium and are needed for them, we said our farewells and they left.

23rd SEPTEMBER

Today we finished putting the clamps in Compartment VII and Compartment VIII. Smit have made the decision that they will use the subfucker by using the rams incorporated on the side of the tool it has not been successful to date. They believe this will do the trick it has not been used in this way in situ yet but the performance of the downward pushing ram does not fill me with confidence. We have been instructed to install the remaining guides and then insert the subfucker, operate the ram and all will be well. Let's hope so this decision is made purely because of the time restraint we are now working under. We have only one more guide to install which should be in by tomorrow; the night shift will get it in. This is a calculated gamble which I hope does not return and bite us on the arse, if we have to take the guides back of to gain access the underside of the holes again we will loose the weather window for sure. The barge is making good progress and will be with us soon!!. I had a funny experience to-day with the Russian doctor who is nicknamed doctor death. This because to date he has had 2 patients one was a sore arm and a cream was prescribed, this gave a severe burning sensation to the patience. Then second patient had a rash in his crotch and unknown to him he was prescribed the same cream which gave him the same result except in a more delicate region. Olga is our interpreter DSND hired for the contract not only translate but listen in to the Russians when they discuss matters, this will enable us to hear all what is said and not just what there interpreters want us to hear. Olga also translates in situation such as above when a patient sea's the doctor. I have not mentioned Olga half as much as I should have, she is invaluable to us and is a perfect lady, and she has dealt with a situation of being offshore with a vessel full of men with great dignity. Her background is, she is a Muscovite living and working as a university lecturer in Edinburgh, this must be some change from her normal way of life. I have been having trouble with my ankle, I am hobbling about like an old man but I do not wish to be another victim of doctor deaths cream, so I am avoiding him. In the mess Olga came up to me and said the doctor is a little upset that I have not sorted his help. I am on good terms with the doctor he also acts as a scribe for the Russians in dive control so I have seen a lot of him over the weeks he is feeling put out. I explain to Olga the story of his previous patients and the burning cream, Olga ever the diplomat asked if I would see him and assured me the cream for the previous is just a coincidence. I reluctantly agreed and said I will see him now, but if he offered me that cream Ill tell him what to do with it. We retired to the doctor's cabin because it was close by, Olga the doctor and me. Once inside I exposed my ankle to his scrutiny. There was some probing and bending of my ankle which was hurting like hell by now. After some deep discussions between Olga and the doc, Olga started to laugh thanks for the sympathy I said, the doctor left the cabin and Olga told me he has some cream that will help. When he came back carrying the same cream as his previous victims had used, he just stared bewilderedly at me and Olga laughing.

24th SEPTEMBER

I was the recipient of a presentation to-day I was called to one side and asked to meet the Admiral in dive control. When I arrived the Admiral appeared with Alexander the interpreter and translated for the Admiral. He thanked me for the work I had put in with the Russian dive team and presented me with a book; it is the same book that was presented to the company representatives on the day of the ceremony commemorating the anniversary of the sinking of the Kursk. Inside is a dedication in Russian and English thanking me for our efforts from the Russian Federation? I must admit I was a bit choked up about that, this ceremony was repeated for the other supervisors. I am glad it was the book I had been trying get a copy from Alexander for a few weeks now all he could say was there were none available, anyway I am well chuffed. We were soon back at work continuing putting in the last guides bolts and torquing them up. That it all the guides are in now let's hope the subfucker does its magic and works. Whether its just optimism but I think it will work this time, no reason I just think it will work this time. We had a false start and a hydraulic hose blew, we will soon change that then its full steam ahead. The barge is about 50 miles away ,its slowed down to give us a little more time to finish these holes, we have agreed to give 12 hours notice for her to come in and set up, she will be using anchor moorings. We have to be along side her for the hook up, we will be in DP(dynamic positioning)this is not a normal operation for us we normally require a minimum stand of requirement for working in close proximity with another vessel, in this case we have to be close to connect up the lifting points to the Kursk. Everyone onboard is now focused for this lift now it's the climax to a lot of work, we believe it will be successful there are no doubters onboard now.

25th SEPTEMBER

Another busy day - we've continued prepping the holes for grippers. We had some subfucking and some grinding to do and we did quite well. We've only got a few holes in Compartment VII and a couple in Compartment VIII to complete. By the time I get up tomorrow I expect it'll be nearly finished, if not finished. The Giant 4 is now about 20 miles away and we should be calling it to move *in soon so we can install the grippers and pick the bugger up. It's getting close to lift time now, getting a bit excited.*

Crew change tomorrow a lot of people are going off. To their dismay they will miss the lift after so much hard work. I wouldn't have thought, nearly three months ago, that we'd be in this position we are in now, but we are. I just hope the weather stays good for us. We're supposed to have a good weather window starting on Thursday. It looks good for bringing in the Giant 4 to set up for the final phase of this job.

26th SEPTEMBER

Quarter to eight in the evening. The crew change took place earlier the last one on this job. Next time we crew change the Kursk should be tucked under the Giant 4 on her way to Murmansk. Its not very often the guys are reluctant to go home they are sad that they will miss the lift.

We have completed the installation of the gripper guides in all the holes now. We now have discovered there is some very large obstruction to clear from section VIII. As I said previously we do not want to have to remove the guide after installation to clear obstructions from the holes. The obstructions turned out to be large electrical cabinets which were at first thought not to be a problem, but now they appear to be. The divers investigated the obstructions and decided they could fit through the guides, just and enter the submarine. The cabinet require unbolting to clear them, we can just lay them on there sides and that should do the trick. It is very eerie being inside the submarine knowing so many men are still inside this steel tomb. We had an unfortunate incident last night; the Russians have people monitoring our cameras constantly. Unfortunately they observed a diver removing plaques from the bulkhead when he was working inside the submarine. I can only think he wanted some kind of souvenir, this is tantamount to robbing the dead not very nice. I was asked to report to there office and asked to explain what had happened. There was no excuse and we apologised for the insult to there dead, it was graciously agreed with the Russians if I talked to the dive team concerned (I did not notice who did this during the dive) that if the articles removed were given to the next team to dive they could replace them back inside the submarine. If this was done no more would be said, all I will say in our companies defence it was not a British or American diver and not employed by DSND. I hope the guy who did this reads it in print we all know who you were, and I hope you are still ashamed to this day!.

We have continued with the clearing of holes and taken some measurements. We are just about there. We are laying down the wire for releasing the suction and may have some work to do on the suction piles but if that's all OK and everybody's happy we're going to bring in the Giant 4 and star the final phase of the operation the lift. We've been under instructions by the engineers as to what to clear inside the holes; Mammoet and Ruben can not agree exactly what has to be removed. Mammoet are taking charge now and they have agreed a little more has to be done but the Giant 4 will come in tomorrow and start to set up. I could be connecting up when I am on shift tomorrow, I hope the weather forecast is good and the decision is made to hook up.

27th SEPTEMBER

Seven o'clock in the evening - shift finished. We finished our work scope inside the Hull about half past nine this morning and moved off sit to let the Giant 4 access to her mooring anchors. The Giant 4 barge is anchoring up right now it should take until midnight before she is moored. When she is in position we have to survey her anchor wires, because we will be working inside her anchor pattern and along side we have to know exactly where they are so we can avoid getting entangled with them. We estimate it will take 5 hours for the ROV to plot the positions of the wires. This will give us some time to go over the hook up sequence and potential dangers to look out for. We have a few little jobs to do before we can hook up, there are Transponder buckets to install which will house the transponders used for the lift, they will relay information to an onboard computer which will inform us if she is lifting level or not. There will be radiation monitors with surface readout placed inside the hull; this will monitor any possible radiation leakage from the reactors if they start to break up during the lift. The worry is the front section is buried in the sea-bed while the aft end is proud of the sea-bed, we do not want the suction to hold down the front section causing more stress in the centre of the lift with the possible consequence of it breaking in two at the point where the reactors are housed. Or the sudden release from the suction at the front causing the submarine to spring up in an uncontrolled manner, again causes more stress in the wrong place with the possibilities of break up. A late check of the forecast predicts a blow over the weekend so the decision the hook up will be delayed until a more favourable weather window. For now all we can do is watch the Giant 4 set up and monitor the weather, this is precisely what I have dreaded. All ready to go but its all down to the weather now, if the winter gales start then that's the end of it, all that hard work gone to waste. I found out the last three hole which were giving us problems were not excepted by Rubens they were by Mammoet so Smit said basically sod them carry on its to late in the day to start arguing. Smit thinking they had the authority over Rubens were brought down to size when we were ordered to go back in and clear some more until Rubens were satisfied, which we did.

As it turned out Rubens refused to sign the acceptance certificate for one hole in particular. It appears to be resolved now whether the certificate is signed or not, I don't know. A bit late in the day to spit the dummy out...

28ᵗʰ SEPTEMBER

Eight o'clock in the evening today's been a rather bitty day. We finished the last couple of jobs on the submarine, we completed the installation of the transponder buckets, we had to place what looked like big bulls eye targets on the outer hull for the ROV to monitor during the lift these will act as reference points during the lift. We also offered up for a trial fit the re-entry rings as they are called. They are a ring of steel with four wires attached, when we fit them up for real they are lowered to us from the Giant 4 and are connected up to the guide buckets, a 60 ton pull is applied. They act not only as a guide for the massive lifting grippers but activate the heave compensators on the barge which require this amount of load to work against. This will enable the grippers to be lowered without any up and down movement from the sea's motion this being a lot safer for the divers to handle and work with. Them trial fit was successful, the previous fears for the bolts on the clams shearing under the tension of 60 ton has evaporated now. Everybody is happy to install the grippers that's all there is left to do now, that and pick her up. There is a rumour gathering momentum that we will have to remain behind after the lift to recover some debris from the sea bed. The engineers will remain and survey the sight to see if there is any debris that might be required to assist them with the investigation of the cause of the accident...

29ᵗʰ SEPTEMBER

We're basically ready to hook it up, but there's a nasty blow due to hit us about midnight: a 60-odd knot wind, so they've decided not to hook it up. We're just moseying about until the weather is right. We support the barge as they want us. We're all just waiting about for somebody to make the big decision. Malcolm (Mammoet) has that responsibility he is a Geordie lad, and everyone is now waiting for Malcolm to say lets go for it. If there is ever a career decision this it, get it right and you are the star of the company get it wrong and the submarine is dropped or breaks up then its the end of your career.

30ᵗʰ SEPTEMBER

Again we're waiting on weather, all ready to hook up They're all getting a bit impatient but the forecast's not good. It's due to come down, but then go straight back up again Obviously it's costing Smit £70-grand a day just for us; even more with the barge sitting there as well. That's quite a lot of money eating into their profits. I expect they'll get twitchy after a couple of days-- they might go for it, who knows?

1ˢᵗ OCTOBER

We were waiting on weather most of the day but at six o'clock the dive team were given permission to dive and start to install the grippers. Malcolm has made the decision to hook up, a brave decision the weather forecast is only good for two days but when I spoke to him he said if we are going to do it, it has to be now... We're starting to install the re-entry rings and when the first gripper came into view it was a sight for sore eyes it marked the beginning of the end for the recovery. The first gripper did not go in easily we had to align the Giant 4 barge on the surface with the kursk on the sea-bed exactly so the grippers were lined up with the holes, we will soon find out if the engineering on the barge and the hole we have made match up perfectly. When we managed to get the first gripper in its hole we had to activate the hydraulics rams which pushed the contact points out from the gripper once that was done the gripper was tensioned to about 10 ton to keep it in place. We think once we get about three or four grippers in place the Giant 4 should be aligned with the kursk and the rest should go in quicker. It now looks like Wednesday for the lift, the weather is starting to rock the vessel a bit we are ok for now, if gets any worse it will cause us problems.

Tomorrow we've got Admiral Popov, the Commander of the Northern Fleet, coming on. And it's rumoured that the Deputy Prime Minister is coming as well as the top men from Mammoet and Smit. Mr Spassky is here he is the top man from Rubens he has been on a while I didn't know who he was, he was very unassuming but very polite. Well there all here now for the big lift, as long as the weather holds and the gripper installation goes to plan hopefully there will be something to see soon.

2ⁿᵈ OCTOBER

Today has been a pretty crappy day really, as I said yesterday we're starting to hook up. We struggled to install the first two grippers they are huge bits of equipment, at the same time as installing we were lining up the barge with the submarine. We have another problem from the barge, seem to work at a slower pace than us their sense of urgency seems to be lacking. I know they are mainly onshore workers and the word from the barge is most of them are sea sick. There does not seem to be a leader over there everything turns into an argument it's very frustrating for us. We have a DSND supervisor on the barge that is used to our way of working, his job is to have things ready before the divers actually need them. This reduces the delay time to a minimum and gets the best out of everybody. Unfortunately he is being ignored right now because one of the owners of Mammoet have a mam onboard the barge and is assuming control. Because is a senior man in the company he has taken control. This is causing us grief its disorganised, they want to perform work we are not ready to for yet, and the work we want to do they don't. We have direct radio link to our man on the barge and he is telling us its chaos on there with this bloke in charge. We will have to sort this out sooner rather than later, time is of the essence right now. The situation right now is we have connected up 5:1 & 5:2 and they are good, 4:9 & 4:10 are connected but are fouled , its costing us precious time un-fouling them with no helpful suggestions on how to do it from the so called experts on the barge. If we can get Craig to take control from this guy we still stand a good chance of lifting this submarine, we are so close right now it's within our grasp. This man causing the problems has been offshore a total of about a fortnight and he thinks he knows how the offshore industry works already. The weather is in the back of our minds all the time here, it will not take much of a change to force us to cancel the lift, the contingency plan for bad weather is to cut the wires and let them fall to the sea-bed if we do this they will not be long enough to re-connect so it would mean the end of the job for this year at least.

3rd OCTOBER

Half past seven in the evening. It's been quite an eventful day. At one point in the afternoon they were talking about abandoning the whole thing because of a very bad weather forecast - saying things like" we have 72 hours to lift it or forget it". It got pretty heated once or twice, but it seems to have died down a bit now. Since we've come so far now, it seems a shame to abandon it. Towards the end of the shift we had seven grippers installed and things were a bit more positive. Admiral Popov and the Director of Rubin Mr Igor Spassky are together overseeing the lift with the company of the CEO's of Smit and Mammoet it's a full house in the top brass department.

4th OCTOBER

The day has consisted of a frustrating time of weather watching, it's picking up just enough to stop us installing the grippers. At six o clock we got the go ahead to continue, there is a problem with the barge, it has heave compensators for the jacks to allow for the vessel movement on the sea. There is only a 2 metre travel which means if the sea state gets above 2metres the weight of the submarine will prematurely come on to the jacks since we only have so far installed 4, instead of the 26 the designers deemed necessary for the lift. There could be a possible overloading of the Jack wires with a consequence of them snapping like twigs. At six o clock the tension was taken up on the already installed jacks and we continued with the installation. You can cut the tension on here with a knife right now it is manifesting itself in unsavoury ways like claims from Smit & Mammoet that its the divers fault for the lack of progress, its not done openly but snidely. The Kursk web site claims that when the divers get to grips with the installation of the grippers it will be a much quicker process. We do not have a problem with the grippers but the barge does, the re-entry rings are made with no tolerance which makes there installation a nightmare. Its not the same trying to install something at 116 metres with the up and down motion of the sea to contend with and a no tolerance fit to boot, as apposed on the surface in a construction yard with as many helping hands as you require. The barge is trying to run the whole show and its not working, they can not see the sub-sea element of the job as we can the personnel on *the Mayo must take control its a shambles right now. I think there are some people trying to make a name for themselves rather than having their full focus on the job in hand. Well that is my rant for the day, I don't know why I am so surprised its always the same in the sub-sea engineering world if anything is going wrong its the divers fault, if it goes well its the top side engineering that's fantastic. The reality is if it was not for these divers we would be a long time back at home by now.*

5th OCTOBER

Eight twenty in the evening, today's been quite a good day. We're now putting in the 16th gripper, 12 to go. We've managed to crack on today hopefully we'll be able to get the grippers installed by tomorrow and lift the sub on Sunday. We had the top echelon from Mammoet and Smit as well as the Admiral, all coming in to dive control to ensure they are part of the final phase. They insisted in talking to the Smit representatives only in Dutch therefore excluding us from the conversation. It may be paranoia but the body language to me says we manage to do this in spite of the Brit divers; our equipment is brilliant it's them who can't operate it. These are the same people who a few days were implying we can't do the job. While they were talking they were also watching the divers trying to install one of their re-entry rings clearly observing the difficulties the divers were having trying to insert the grippers with little or no tolerance. They didn't mention that or even bothered to asked us why we were having difficulties. I am sure the taste of success was on their lips and more was on order.

What else has happened? We've just been cracking on and seem to have got the barge people into a bit of routine now, starting to think ahead to the next step. Craig has taken control and it's paying dividends. This time tomorrow I should be able to say we're nearly done. The sweepstake is still on. My slot is ten o'clock tomorrow evening. It might be slightly optimistic but I think it'll be ready as long as nothing goes wrong this evening. Then the Mayo will move of to a safe distance and monitor the lift with the ROV.

6th OCTOBER

Eight o'clock in the evening and we've had a good day. We've cracked on, got a lot sorted and I'd be surprised if we are not ready to pick this thing up by tomorrow. The divers have pegged down a DSND flag to the submarine to the outer hull just in front of the conning tower. Due to the lack of recognition we feel that has not been afforded to us, the flag will be one of the first things that will be seen by the worlds press when they dewater the Kursk in dry dock in Murmansk. I believe it is part of the contract between DSND Smit and Mammoet that we are not allowed to get any publicity from this project all that belongs to them. All the dignitaries are here now waiting for the success to wash over them. I was told the Deputy Prime Minister of Russia was to be onboard for the Lift but apparently protocol for bids this. Apparently the Prime minister must have a minimum amount of guards with him at all times and we can't accommodate that many on the vessel due to the life boat situation(there must be a life boat seat for everyone onboard at any one time). Instead he will stay on the battleship "Peter the Great" she is just standing of our Stbd side. With luck we will lift her tomorrow and she will make her way to Roslyakovo towed at a speed of 4km per hour for the 195km journey. She will then rendezvous with the Russian dry dock; two auxiliary pontoons will be attached to the Giant 4. The Giant 4 & the Kursk will be ballasted up to until the Kursk has enough clearance to enter the flooded dry dock. Once inside the dry dock the Kursk will be lower to the bottom of the dry dock and released from the Giant 4, the Giant 4 will then vacate the dry dock her task complete, the dry dock can then be de-

watered given access to the surface crews who have the sad task of locating the stricken bodies of the lost crew, and deal with the reactors and armaments to make it safe. It doesn't seem like three months have passed since we started out on this mission, and now we are at the stage were we are going to lift her. Everything is ready the radiation monitors have been placed inside of the hull, the transponders are in place to monitor the level ness of the submarine during the lift. There is a computer readout relayed from the Giant 4 from the lifting jack telling us what load each jack is experiencing, the computer will control the jacks so an even distribution is applied to each jack. The world press are standing by as you can imagine, either to report the success or the biggest catastrophe since the Hiroshima bomb blast lets hope its not the latter, not that we would know much about it. When she is lifted and on her way we have been informed we will have about 24 hours work to lift the debris the engineers want recovered for the investigation. After that it will be back to Kirkeness de-mobilisation of equipment and personnel, and a big piss up in the town.

7th OCTOBER

Still waiting were just about there now just a few inspections to see if there are any problems that might arise. During the ROV survey Smit noticed the flag and went ballistic, they demanded that we dived and removed the flag with the threat of back charging the company for the time it took to remove it. One she is lifted we have to install a net over the front to stop any loose object falling out during the tow into Murmansk that will be the last job for us to do on the submarine itself. Everything is ready now all Malcolm has to say is lift and the accumulation of months of work will either be successful or failure we will know soon.

8th OCTOBER

TODAY HAS BEEN THE DAY! *At 3:55 this morning the "Kursk" was lifted off the seabed with no problems whatsoever. All the anticipated problems with the suction never manifested themselves the drag wire was not used or required she lifted just like it was meant to happen it was an eerie sight to see her lift slowly the lifting jack readouts did not indicate any problems, it took 9600 tons of lift just a little over what was calculated for the section to be lifted weighs, there was a cloud of sediment which caused the ROV to loose sight for a while and that was the only small hiccup. All I can say the feeling of euphoria was thick on the boat at that moment we all stood about like grinning Cheshire cats. I wandered up to the Russian Federations office to speak to the Navy lads who we have grown to like very much during the recovery. It was a sight to see they were a very happy bunch of people; there was lots of hugging and back slapping. Sergei the chief engineer of the Kursk (the crew lost in the Kursk were hi friends and colleagues) came up to me he was full of emotion not far from crying and said "thank you for doing this for us" and hugged me, this coming from him was very special and something I will never forget. I left them to celebrate together it also means the divers can keep their promise made and written on the scroll place in the submarine, to recover it only when the Kursk is in her home port and the bodies are recovered. Once the Kursk was about 20 metres above sea-bed the Giant 4 started to slip her moorings. This surprised me I would have thought they would have needed her fully up under the hull and secure before they left. I spoke to one of the salvage experts about this and he said " no with the tow being so slow they can work with no problem and it will save time because the rate of accent it will take along time for the Kursk to be under the Giant 4 we can be well on the way in the time it will take". As she was slipping her moorings the battleship Peter the Great sailed close by with her horns blaring. The deck was lined with Russian Navy Crew waving at us and a loud speaker was blasting out somebody making a speech. I turned to Alexander the interpreter and asked him what that was all about, he told me it was President Putin speaking directly from the Kremlin I am not sure if he was pulling my leg or not??. It's been a great day al the dignitaries now want of our vessel and on to the giant 4 now she is the star of the moment. One small snag the weather is not permitting helicopters to take off from Murmansk there is a blizzard in progress. Not to be beaten they want to be transferred in our rubber zodiac boat to a supply boat which will catch up with the Giant4, my lasting impression of these dignitaries is them in the rubber boat chasing the Giant 4 not wanting to be left behind. We are left to recover the pumps off the suction anchors, which belong to Smit, they will have to be burned of it will save Smit some money. Contractually we've got 15 lifts from the sea-bed for Rubin. We are waiting for them to decide what they want us to recover for them. This shouldn't take too long we should be on our way soon.*

9th OCTOBER

It's half past seven in the evening we will be sailing for Kirkeness soon. The job's done, everything's finished it feels funny all the tension and pressure of the last few days have evaporated. That's it the end of the recovery it's a weird feeling just a couple of dives to do to complete the job. The lift was easy, nothing to it - it just came up - a bit of an anti climax. The Russians just left a helicopter came they all got on and left it's like they were never there. I went up to the departure lounge to say goodbye I was very sad to see them all leave. They were all in their formal Navy dress very smart, Sergei(Kursk chief engineer) came up to me and said goodbye, I joked he was not wearing the Yorkshire rose pin I gave him adding he promised he would always wear. He said he was very sorry and went to his bag and retrieved it and placed it on his uniform next to his military medals, He gave me a perfect salute shook my hand and was gone. The doctor left with a large oversized luggage, a lot more than he came with. There was not much left in the ships hospital though, nobody is bothered things are hard to come by for the Russians; I expect they must get what they can when they can. Now everybody has left its back to the final stage of the job, messing about with the pumps on the suction anchors we had problems cutting them of we have access difficulties, there is also a problem with blowbacks from the burning. We have appealed to Smit to leave them and eventually they agreed. It was our last dive on the Kursk the divers were Phil Freeman and Steve Ley our company had commissioned a memorial stone to lay on the site of the Kursk in memory of those who lost there life. There was no input from the Russians, Smit or Mammoet I don't think they were even aware of what we had intended to do. During this ceremony we lowered the stone which was engraved half in Russian the other in English. It was laid with two wreaths and the ROV captured this on video, what it could not capture was the poem Steve recited as he laid the wreath it was by an unknown author it read so **DO NOT STAND BY MY GRAVE AND WEEP, I AM NOT THERE, I DO NOT SLEEP I AM A THOUSAND WINDS THAT BLOW I AM A DIAMOND GLINT ON SNOW I AM THE SUNLIGHT ON A RIPENED GRAIN I AM THE GENTLE AUTUMN RAIN WHEN YOU AWAKE IN THE MORNING HUSH I AM THE SWIFT UPLIFTING RUSH OF QUIET BIRDS IN CIRCLING FLIGHT I AM THE SOFT STAR SHINE AT NIGHT DO NOT STAND BY MY GRAVE AND CRY, I AM NOT THERE I DID NOT DIE.** *These were just the right words for the occasion we concluded with a minute's silence.* This particular piece of video was shown on Dutch television a few days later, some reporters from a Dutch TV channel were allowed onboard in Kirkeness I not sure how they managed to get the video footage of the ceremony. Smit went ballistic again because they did not know anything about this ceremony, they must have looked like idiots when it was shown and their press department could not answer any questions about it. Smit demanded the tape with the threat of withholding payment for the vessel hire unless it is produced quickly. They even used a picture of the 2 divers holding the wreath in there official book of the salvage operation, hypocrisy or what. *We set sail about six we're heading for Kirkenes, hopefully Smit and Mammoet will take us all out for a well deserved beer, and this is a promise made by Malcolm. My last unenviable task is to announce the Barent Sea crib champion, I am so tempted to say me but alas Fitzsimmons will never let me live it down. The competition has been aggressively fought over but Anthony Fitzsimmons is the outright winner, luck and the use of mirrors was his main tactics.*

10th OCTOBER

It has been a hectic day we have TV crews and reporters running wild all over the ship trying to get interviews with anyone who will stop and talk to them. We have choice between Germany, Holland & Norwegian television. I was asked along with Basher Bates to accompany the German crew who were doing a documentary, But Basher being far more photogenic than me took centre stage and I left them to it. We had a local reporter from Kirkeness daily who was given full access to the vessel and crew, I expect it will be the biggest story his paper will cover. In amongst all this commotion we are still trying to de-mobilise equipment and remobilise equipment which we stored in Kirkeness like gas quads. The ship is intent on sailing tomorrow. We have our company boss flying out to-day to congratulate us on our achievement should be a good party to-night. I spoke to Malcolm about the crew that finish at mid-day; he said he would make sure some money is put behind the bar for them in the afternoon. Everyone else will meet in the same bar later tonight. Tomorrow is home time I am looking forward to that; we are expecting our flight details any time now.

11th OCTOBER

Nine o'clock in the morning - a heavy night last night. It was a very disappointing that the people from Smit & Mommoet who've been saying we'd done a wonderful job for them, could not be bothered to spend any time with us. My suspicions were aroused when we met the early shift in town; they said no money was forthcoming from Smit or Mammoet for a drink. Much later they did grace us with their company just in time for the last orders in the bar where they offered to buy us a beer, this was after they themselves had a slap up celebratory dinner in the best restaurant in town well away from us. I was very angry and told them to shove there drink, I do not believe they could have been so insensitive. There will be plenty of time for them to celebrate in style, a few hours of there time to thank the men who put so much effort in for them. I think Smit & Mammoets true colours were shown that night and they were not nice. I am sure those companies will squeeze every drop of PR from this salvage, I was talking to a Smit representative a couple of days ago about how much money they have made from this, the answered surprised me he said its cost them a couple of million dollars, which is peanuts to the amount of prestige and advertising its given them for their companies, he continued you could not buy this kind of publicity. It has left a sour taste in the mouth, they did not have the good grace to acknowledge the divers who on more than one occasion rescued this project from failure. I just want to go home, but before we can fly home we have to pay a visit to a doctor who has been ensconced in the local hotel waiting for our arrival. We were a bit bewildered why we have to see a doctor before we could go home. On arrival at the hotel it was explained to us that blood was to be taken from us and will be stored at some facility somewhere for our long term health protection. The blood sample will be tested for any abnormalities; a sample will be kept in case any time in the future we suffer from any health problems which could be attributed to the Kursk project. We will have documented evidence of our health at the time of the project, and this evidence could be called on in any court action if required. Once we had all been seen by the doctor we boarded the bus to take us to the airport. We had a couple of hours wait for our flight to Oslo; a few sore heads were in evidence mine included. Passing through customs our baggage was thoroughly searched for Items not permitted on the flight; with the improved security alert since 9/11 nail files and toe nail clippers were considered as weapons. It seemed ironic to us after what we had just been through the last couple of months, now our nail files are considered dangerous. The flight was uneventful it was nice to be on our way home, when we arrived at Oslo we went our own separate ways to different parts of UK and some cases Europe. The problem we had at Oslo though was the flight schedules we had gave us little or no time to get to the departure lounges for our onward flights. All you could see was a mass of guys running down the departure lounge gangway shouting see ya to each other as we tried to make our flight connections, a very undignified way for it to end.

I only recently found out that when we were about to lift the Kursk the Americans have invaded Afghanistan. How ironic and sad this world we live in is, we have spent so much time and effort into recovering this stricken submarine and the poor souls onboard. Then the leaders of the most powerful nation in the world have decided to start another conflict on the other side of the world. We recover one war machine of mass destruction while another kicks of elsewhere. Very sad makes you wonder if it was all worth it.

After the submarine's mooring in Murmansk investigations into its condition began in earnest. Eventually a total of 69 bodies were recovered from its interior.

By the end of November 2001 there were several changes within the top ranks of the Russian Naval command. One of the first casualties was Admiral Popov. According to BBC Online of 1st December, he had been demoted, and several other officers had been dismissed, ostensibly not for the events surrounding the "Kursk" disaster as such. There had been "serious failures in the organisation of the military training activities of the fleet, claimed the C-in-C of the Russian Navy Vladimir Kuroyedov. The attempted distancing from the "Kursk" was further emphasised by the fact that on the very day Admiral Kuroyedov made his statement President Putin announced that he had received an official report which said that it was still too early to say what caused the disaster. The President, however, did concede that the "collision with a foreign submarine" theory was dead. Or as he put it: "looked shaky".

In December, too, there was an outpouring of nationalistic pride at the success of the "recovery". Two Russian commentators Semyon Maisterman, from the news agency Itar-Tass, told the popular magazine Itogi that the feat of raising the stricken vessel had been an almost exclusive Russian affair! Russia, they claimed, had completed a task that had never been accomplished before in the history of the world's undersea fleet. This demonstrated, they continued, their country's capacity to amaze the rest of the world. Only one of the world's lost nuclear submarines had been raised from the deep - and Russia had done it!! It had hoisted the submarine, complete with reactors and ammunition, without mishap. Radioactive material might have leaked from the vessel at any moment and an explosion, had it occurred, would have blasted Giant 4 and the naval escort "to atoms". It praised those, "the heroes", who had, at a depth of 100 metres, "virtually scratched the "Kursk" out of the mud with their bare hands". Perhaps one can make allowances for such high-flown nationalist hyperbole, but the one-sided claims are obviously fanciful.

The reporters then lauded President Putin for his resolution not to be daunted "a year ago" and "for failing to spread ashes on his head...for the loss of the "Kursk". "Thank God he didn't. Putin did a much stronger thing, assuming not the blame, but the responsibility for the further fate of the "Kursk". "Russia is an amazing nation", crowed the writers. "Amazing by reason of its unpredictability". Possibly it is the principal trait that distinguishes a superpower - being able to constantly amaze the rest of the world".

The initiative for the recovery of the "Kursk" came mainly from the Russians; it is true, though not for entirely altruistic reasons. Rather it was motivated by a mixture of fear -- for the environmental consequences; public outcry -- for the retrieval of the corpses; and also pressure from the military establishment -- to reclaim the weapons and advanced technology on board , before any foreign nations could lay their hands on such material. But the diving and lifting technology required, indeed, much of the skilled manpower and expertise for preparing, lifting and transporting the stricken vessel came from outside the Russian Federation. The Netherlands, principally, with its depth of expertise in lifting and transporting such a huge object from such a depth, must receive the lion's share of the accolades. Divers and cutters from Britain and Norway had the experience and expertise to see through the arduous work of preparing the hull for lifting. Admiral Verich admitted as much when he said, at a reception in Aberdeen, after the "Mayo" returned there, that the success of the mission was due to the "exceptional professionalism of the participants in the work"

Meanwhile the investigation into the actual causes of the sinking was well underway under the aegis of the Prosecutop - General Vladimir Ustinov. In an interview with website strana.ru's correspondent he was asked whether the raising of the "Kursk" would help reveal the truth about its sinking. "Of course it will", he stated confidently, though he admitted that "the materials we have collected so far cannot provide a complete and totally clear picture of the event". Mr Ustinov confirmed that his office was working closely with the Commission set up under Me Klebanov and he added that he had the best investigative and legal minds at his disposal - top experts, still young, but highly professional. Eight teams were engaged in sifting through every aspect of the state of the fabric, the instrument readings, and so on, in order to obtain a total picture of the submarine at the precise moment of the disaster. The examination of the bodies of the victims would show the causes of their deaths, the Prosecutor-General said. But the full picture would be incomplete until they raised the submarine's bow section. Mr Ustinov, like his President, did his part to lay the "collision" theory to rest. All the ships that were in the area at the time of the disaster had been examined - "no traces of a collision have been found on them," he affirmed. Finally he re-iterated Russia's determination to be open to scrutiny during the investigation: "we will be maximally open, but certainly not to the detriment of the interests of our country and the state.

Almost simultaneously with all these developments Admiral Kuroyedov announced that Russia had decided to raise the forward section in 2002. Surprisingly, however, he went on to declare that to do it "no foreign divers and facilities will, be necessary". (As we shall see matters do not seem to be proceeding exactly along that track.) Another senior naval commander added that, in the meantime, the site of the shattered bow would be closed: not for the sake of secrecy, but for security. Furthermore no fishing would be allowed in the area.

When writing this book I tried to tell you how it was as truthfully as possible, I also wanted to give an insight of how we do our business offshore. To this end I have asked Mark Girdlestone who was chosen to be a member of one of the Russian dive team. Because of the technical equipment we use and the familiarisation of our emergency drills it was deemed necessary to insist that the Russian dive team in saturation will include a British diver. His sole job will be to remain in the bell and monitor the Russian divers and he could be called on in the event of an emergency, this was a compromise we insisted on before we would agree to put the Russians in sat. We thought Mark had the temperament for this task, knowing it will be very boring being the bellman every day. His patience will be tested working with divers who will have trouble communicating with him. To this end I have asked Mark if he will give me a contribution to this book on his unique experience he had on the project.

PHOTOS

SPACE BETWEEN HULLS WHICH DIVERS HAD TO CLEAR

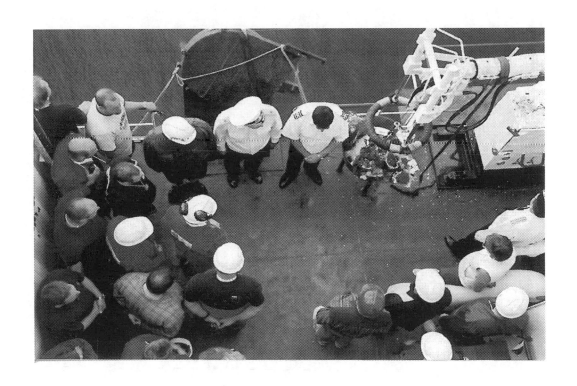

MEMORIAL SERVICE AT THE TRAGEDY SITE

HELICOPTER CREW CHANGE DAY

MAYO FULL DECK BEFORE WE LEAVE KIRKENES FOR THE KURSK WORK SITE

SUITS AGAINST NUCLEAR CONTAMINATION

PETER THE GREAT RUSSIAN FLAGSHIP AND GUARD BOAT

HOSPITAL SHIP ON STANDBY

SCENES OF DEVASTATION THE KURSK HAD SUFFERED

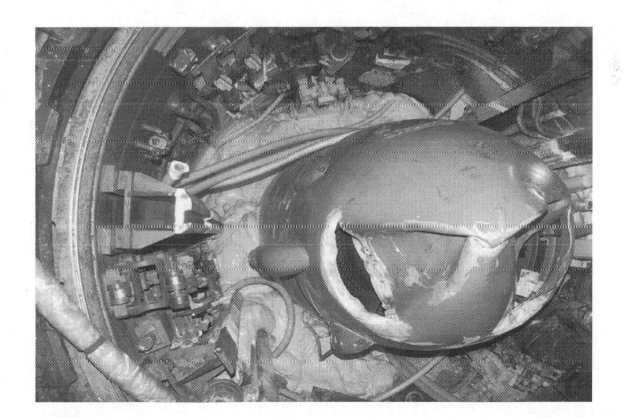

DIVERS PREPARING THE SUBMARINE FOR LIFTING

CUTTING OF THE FRONT SECTION OF THE KURSK
SO IT CAN BE RECOVERED TO THE DRY DOCK

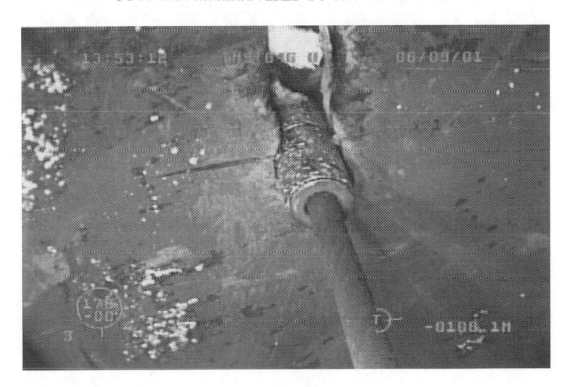

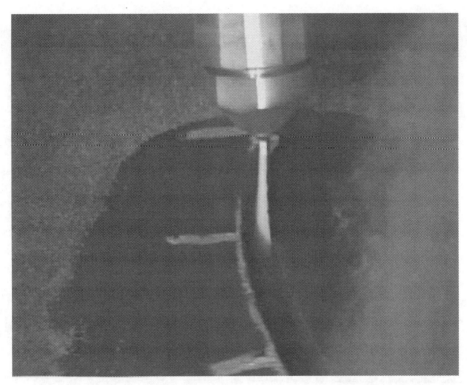

CUTTING THE PRESSURE HULL FOR THE GRIPPERS

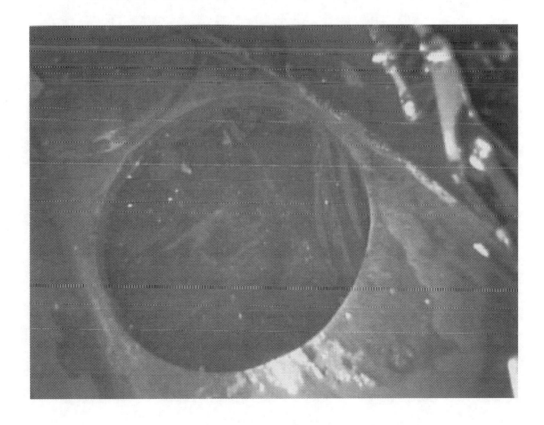

HOLE CUT READY FOR THE GUIDE AND GRIPPER

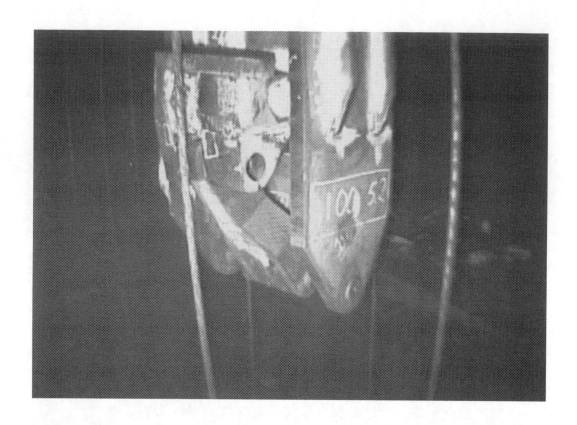

GRIPPER ABOUT TO BE INSERTED INTO THE HOLES

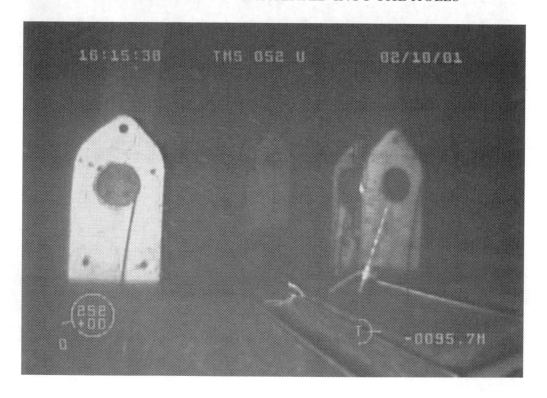

GRIPPERS IN PLACE READY FOR THE LIFT

CONNING TOWER WHERE SCROLL WAS PLACED

READY FOR THE LIFT

MEMORIAL STONE LEFT AT WORK SITE

RUSSIAN DIVE TEAM

DIVERS WORKING ON THE JOB

WALLY AND FRIEND

A CHURCH WE VISITED

SUMMER PALACE

WINTER PLACE

WALLY AND ALEC AT THE RUSSIAN EMBASSY RE-
CEIVING THE ORDER OF FRIENDSHIP

WALLY MEETS PRESIDENT PUTIN

MARK'S STORY

Even though I am an ex R.N Clearance Diver, having served during the cold war, I have always held the view that 'Jaw, jaw is better than war, war'. Consequently when asked if I would join the Russian Dive Team, I accepted, for two reasons; firstly, it was an opportunity to hold out a genuine hand of friendship to a bewildered nation and secondly it was a sense of curiosity on my part as to how these guys' minds worked. It was an opportunity to find out who the enigmatic Russian people really are.

I was acutely aware of the Russians' sense of unease at my being there to 'nanny' them and I understood this because they were competent divers in their own field; albeit attacking and sinking enemy ships, rather than carrying out salvage or underwater engineering. However, a mutual sense of confidence gradually emerged, partly due to our confined living space, and partly because we all felt the irony of the situation we found ourselves in and decided that we would best cope with it through sharing humour wherever and when ever we could.

Prior to actually being 'blown down' to the working depth, the Russian divers had undergone surface safety training which they undertook seriously and thoroughly, much to their credit. But their sense of gravitas cracked when they were required to watch a rather outdated Royal Navy video about saturation diving. Much to their amusement, it featured non other than yours truly who was then aged twenty two, slim, fresh-faced and sporting a head of curly hair! Now nearly double that age, I was only just about recognisable to the Russians and I could see by their reaction that they were bemusedly noting the heavy toll that over twenty years of saturation diving has on one's good looks! The Russians were now as curious about me as I was about them.

Having been assured that I would have another sat dive at a later date, where I could actually work on the sub itself, on 21st July I found myself along with two Russian divers, Igor and Sergei, being blown down to a depth of 108 meters. I was given the impression that the Russians spoke little or no English so I had hastily crafted a slip of paper on which were written basic Russian words and phrases such as 'go right' and 'go left'. However, during the meal breaks, I noticed the lads eagerly pouring over the ship's menu which was of course written in English. They seemed suspiciously good at deciphering the options. My suspicion that they could indeed read and speak English was upheld after a feeble attempt on my part to explain with the use of utterly comical hand and facial gestures, that they were mistaken in thinking food would be scarce and that there really was no need to hide trays of food around the Diving Chamber; they could have a meal whenever they wished. The relief of the Russian divers, upon knowing that they would be well fed for the next few weeks, resulted in them dropping their guard and they lightened up considerably. They began to talk to me in broken English about their careers, their hobbies and their families back on the mainland as well as their sadness at the loss of the Kursk.

Saturation Divers spend long weeks living together in very confined conditions in a Chamber the size of a bathroom and a camaraderie develops, whether you're Russian or English and it soon became clear to me just how much the Russian lads had been deeply effected by the loss of the Kursk.

During the first Bell run, Sergei leapt from the Bell and landed in (and I mean in!) the front end of the submarine where the wreckage was. I could hear he was very distressed and that Igor was speaking frantically on the comms. to the Russian Supervisor who was located on the Mayo. Between us, we got Sergei back to the Bell where I could see he was extremely distraught, but the Russian Supervisor was asking him to return to work. At this point I intervened; Sergei was in no fit mental state to carry on and I relayed the problem to British Diving Supervisor, Adrian Ladd. The decision was made to get the Bell back and once Sergei was in the Chamber rather than the Bell, he spoke in English. He and Igor told me that he, Sergei, had actually served on the Kursk and that friends were on board that had been killed. Even though he had bravely wanted to help recover the sub. his courage had understandably failed as he fell through the wreckage into the nightmarish debris. He was just too personally associated with the dreadful accident to carry on and a decision was made to decompress him.

It was a sobering incident for all of us but the work had to carry on and later that day another Russian diver was blown in to sat whose name was Sergei, also. And so the weeks passed. Each Bell run I was on standby for an emergency rescue if needed, monitoring the two Russian divers as they worked. After each shift, the Bell came back to the Chamber where I would help them out of their diving suits and generally look after them. We would then talk about their dive in the unspoken knowledge that they were only a few feet away from where their colleagues had died. But then the conversation gradually lightened and we would talk once more of families and of favourite food and drink, usually over mug of coffee, wherein Igor would stir seven teaspoons of sugar. He had a particularly sweet tooth!

We watched a few Russian language films during the decompression and they were all comedies. This was, apparently, the usual genre of Russian films, so I felt acutely embarrassed when Anglo/American films were shown because they tended to be action films portraying the Russians as the 'dark enemy'. The lads were visibly shocked by this: They had never considered themselves as the bad guys. I too, had stopped thinking of them as the 'bad guys', 'the enemy'; they were now my friends. It was as the events of 9/11 unfolded that they went out of their way to show me that they considered me their friend also.

A few weeks after completing the sat dive with the Russian lads, I took some leave and then returned into sat as promised, to work on the Kursk herself. It was during the final part of the salvage that the terrorist attack on the USA happened. Although I was in the Chamber when events unfolded, like the rest of the world, I was shocked beyond belief. Both Igor and Sergei were still on board the Mayo and they made a point of coming down to speak to me through the porthole to express their distress as best they could. They tried very hard to find words in English to tell me that even though the Americans and we Brits by association was traditionally their enemy, they empathised with our feelings of hurt and incomprehension at such an act and that they felt great sympathy for me, their friend. I was deeply moved at this and although I will never forget where I was at the time 9/11 took place, I will also never forget the gesture of respect from the Russian Divers. Upon reflection it seems to me that for the most, people are the same the world over. We all prefer peace to war. We all want to protect our families and friends, we're all proud people but if given a chance we will try to find common grounds for friendship. By this act of terror we were all forced to re-examine who or what the enemy was: I didn't know anymore and neither did they. But one thing we did know for sure was that Mark, Sergei and Igor were friends, because we had all shared an incredible experience. 'Up on the door! Igor and Sergei, I will never forget you!'

*****

I have also taken the opportunity to ask Wally Wallace the OPM (Offshore Project Manager) his insight to the job. Wally was invited with the Captain Alec Macleod to visit Moscow and meet President Putin who wished to thank the project team for their work.

WALLY'S STORY

On 12th August 2000 in the Barents Sea there was an incident on the Russian submarine Kursk which would have an unforeseeable effect on the lives of a great many people.

The Kursk was sunk by a huge explosion in the fore end of the submarine which sent her to the sea bed with the loss of all on board.

Obviously those who lost loved ones would be traumatically effected, others like myself though would take from it a great deal of memorable and positive memories.

I as a younger man through the sixties and early seventies had spent time in the forces, it being the time of the cold war most of our training had been geared to fighting the Soviet Union. At that time I would not have been able to perceive any way that some twenty five years later I would be in the Kremlin meeting the Russian President Vladimir Putin, but that is what happened.

After the initial shock of the incident and a considerable amount of political manoeuvring it was decided by President Putin that Kursk would be recovered. Negotiations were held between the Russians and Mammoet a Dutch specialist lifting company who also recruited the help of Smit International famed Salvage Company who would be needed to supply the lifting barge. On completion of these negotiations and final agreement work moved on at a pace. Specialist cutting company, Radiation detection and Diving services were contracted in.

It was at this time that our involvement was confirmed, I was then offshore manager on DSND Mayo a diving support vessel operating mostly in the North Sea, *although our expertise is in oil field support we set about planning for our needs for lifting the Kursk.*

It was now May of 2001 and one of the requirements of the contract was that Kursk would be lifted by the end of the year, so time was not on our side. Preparation for the Kursk job continued in parallel with Mayo continuing with her duties in the North Sea. Some of the lads were able to visit a sister vessel of the Kursk which proved very helpful later in the project, the consistency between the vessels was amazing.

My first dealings with the Russians was when a group of them came to Aberdeen to join our project risk assessment, not the normal run of the mill risk assessment but a couple of days worth attended by some eminent radiation experts, and many others.

Preparations ready I met the Russian crew at Aberdeen Airport on 3rd July, took them to Stone haven for a customary welcome pint and then on to Aberdeen Harbour for their first acquaint with Mayo and her crew. That night the Russian team spent in one of Aberdeen's hotels before joining the vessel to set sail for the project on 4th July 2001. In order to achieve our goal we were going to need things to go well technically and more importantly we were going to need good luck with the weather, fortunately we were going to get both.

By the end of the first week of October the job was complete and Kursk was safely on her way to Sorvo??? With the departure of the Kursk Mayo spent a couple of days clearing the site and laying a commemorative stone before departing to Kirkeness where we picked up equipment before starting the long journey back to Aberdeen.

Once safely home we were joined again by a number of our Russian friends and were hosted at a reception by the Lady Sherriff???? We discovered at this time that the Russian expertise with vodka is fairly well matched by their abilities with Whisky.

It was in November of 2001 that I along with Alec Macleod Captain of Mayo and our wives were invited to visit Moscow, the trip did not start well for me and Jennifer as we were in Moscow and our luggage was still in Amsterdam, it is not easy to pick up a replacement Kilt in Moscow.
During our stay I was privileged to be invited to the Kremlin, and met with president Putin, and several other Russian dignitaries it was a huge honour and an experience of a life time, particularly when I was informed that we were to receive an award for the works we had carried out.
I am in no way an expert but it is plain to see even to the untrained eye that the art work and craftsmanship of the building are exemplary.

The evening reception was lubricated with copious amounts of vodka, a fact to which Jennifer bore witness the following day; in fact she witnessed it several times the following day.

Our next meeting with our Russian friends was in St Petersburg, where we staged a reunion weekend. An amazing city of huge historic interest and fantastic museums and churches and of course yet again not a little bit of vodka.

Lastly I again along with Captain Macleod was invited to the Russian Embassy in London where we received the Order of Friendship of the Russian Federation, an honour I certainly do not personally deserve, I do believe though that the Team from Mayo both offshore and onshore support are worthy of this recognition and take this opportunity to thank them all once again for making this happen and allowing me these great experiences.

It must never be forgotten that all this stemmed from a massive tragedy and our thoughts will remain forever with those who were lost and those they left behind on that fateful day.

*****

It is now early January 2002 and we are back into our usual routine, working for the oil companies In the North Sea. I still think a lot about the salvage of the Kursk. The Russian Navy were invited over to Aberdeen for a civic reception, unfortunately I could not attend. Hearing how nice it was to see our Russian friends again from those who did attend, started me thinking of the possibilities of visiting their Navel base in St Petersburg which is also where the Rubin Design Bureau head office is based. I put the word out around the vessel to find out if there was any interest for the visit and the initial response was very good. With this support for the visit I started to plan and organise the trip. I naively thought this would be fairly simple process, find a plane going to St Petersburg, book a hotel and go. As it turned out it was a complicated mission, which was only accomplished with the help of Olga our translator on the salvage operation. I managed to get Olga's e-mail address and told her of our intended visit, which she thought was a good idea and offered to help in any way she could. Fortunately Olga had made good friends with the Russian contingent and was still keeping in touch with them, I had a telephone number of Andrei (a diver) who was based there, and Mark was also in contact with the divers he was in sat with. Their reactions to our suggestion were very positive and were looking forward to seeing us in the near future. Olga also offered to help in attaining the visa's which I had forgotten would be required, she also got in touch with Mr Spassky the head of the Ruben Design Bureau and asked if they would be interested in helping with the visit which he was. With all the positive feedback I thought this will have to happen, my first main task was to get firm commitments from people for that I needed to get dates and costs. I did ask the company for any help with the funding, they had funded the Russian Navy to come to Aberdeen so it was politely refused, they did agree on financing a wreath for us to take with us to lay at the cemetery where the Kursk casualties are laid to rest, it is my intentions during the visit to pay our respects to the casualties at their final place of rest.

After a while Olga e-mailed me and told me that she had contacted the Russian Embassy and with the influence of her friends in Russia the Visa fee would be wavered for our trip, we just had to put Kursk visit on our application form and it will be taken care of. Armed with my list of the lads who had committed to go I approached the airlines to see if I could get a discounted flight for our party. I was not very successful but British Airways did give us a group discount which helped keep the cost down. My only other problem was accommodation, Olga again came to the rescue and got in touch with Rubin who offered to organise a hotel they use for foreign guests visiting their offices they could get us discounted rooms no problem. That put everything in place the date was confirmed 8th of March, all the lads had to do was pay for their flight in advanced and the trip was on. Adrian Ladd, Jimmy Irvine, Wally Wallace, Olga, Mark Girdlestone. Paul Mcque, John Sheppard, Phil Freeman, Dave King, John Gratton and Andy Pybus were the motley crew, we did not know what to expect but we were looking forward to the visit.

The date of the visit soon came around, the plan was for us to make our own way to Gatwick airport and meet in the departure lounge bar when I arrived John Sheppard was there and we ordered ourselves a beer as the rest arrived the more the beer flowed we had two no shows, Andy Pybus and John Gratton after a quick telephone call they told us they had not received their passports back from the Embassy in time but hoped to have them by tomorrow. Their intended to fly out on the Saturday make their own way to the hotel. The announcement was made for us to go to our departure gate for our flight to St Petersburg and before we knew it we were in the air enjoying another beer on our way not really knowing what to expect when we get there, will there be someone there to greet us will we be able to get a taxi to the hotel will anyone understand us thankfully we had Olga to help us with the language.

When we arrived it was all a bit of a blur when we got to the customs gate and was identified as the Kursk salvage visiting team we were ushered through the VIP route no customs for us we went through a couple of doors, when we emerged on the other side it was unreal there were television crews and interviewers they started asking us questions and jostling for our attention and in the middle like a giant in full dress uniform was Andrei who gave us all a bear hug, there were others to all hugging and shaking our hands I was overwhelmed I couldn't believe the amount of people there to greet us . Andrei herded us onto a waiting bus outside and as soon as we were seated we were given a beaker each and it was filled with neat vodka, we had to drink it in one gulp as is the custom they told us. We drank 5 bottles of vodka in the time it took us to reach the hotel; we soon discovered that this will be the normal activities for the rest of the visit. There were time during the visit that I tried to substitute water for vodka but they always discovered my ruse and refilled to the brim with vodka and insisted it was to be downed in one. Andrei, Igor .Sergie and the rest of the Russians also drank drink for drink, but it did not seem to affect them at all. We were given a brief time to check in the hotel and dump our bags in our rooms. We were then to make our way to the bar to meet and greet our hosts, it was very nice to meet them all again some had travelled along way and the Navy had given them permission to be with us for the duration of our visit. We were ushered back onto the bus and a tour of the city was the plan this was accompanied with the obligatory bottles of vodka by now we pretty well sozzled. Because of the language difficulty they provide us with a professional tour guide called Olga funny enough, she was very good and seems to know everything about everything. I am not quite sure of the places we visited I remember going into a magnificent church the paintings on the walls and ceilings were fantastic and the architecture was brilliant too. When we emerged there was a man dressed in 17th century costume and he put his arm around Wally and we took his picture, it was his way of making a few dollars of the tourist as we were about to pay him Andrei took him to one side and explained who we were, he would not take any money from us as he considered us hero's of the Russia for what we did. As we found out everyone we met thought this and we were treated with the utmost respect. When we eventually returned to our hotel we met in the bar and the vodka was still flowing, Phil by this time had reached his limit, with the travel and little sleep he slumped at the bar and the Russian were concerned for him we put him to bed, There were still a couple of the lads wanting to carry on and they were took on the town I had had enough by then and went to bed

In the morning when I awoke nursing a very large hangover after a quick shower I went down to breakfast you had to pass by the bar to reach the dinning room, at the bar were still a couple of the Russian lads still drinking vodka they told me that they had only just returned from the town an hour before and were waiting for us to start again, at this point of time they thrust another full glass of vodka in my hand and insisted I drank it. Not wishing to offend I did and it was the worst thing I could have done at this point in time I nearly threw up there and then, I managed to make back to my room.

The plan was to meet in the foyer at about nine and we would visit the cemetery for the laying of the wreath I had brought from UK. The rest of the lads turned up in dribs and drabs looking the worst for their night out lots of headaches that morning. The Admiral and the rest of the Team from the naval side turned up to and we boarded the bus together and made our way to the cemetery it was very cold morning and Andrei advised me to wear a coat at which I said I would be fine, I wish I had taken his advice it was bitter. When we arrived at the cemetery we had to walk to the graves it is a very big cemetery and there is an area assigned to the Kursk crew there were many wreaths there and some of the graves had pictures of the victims within. There was a television crew there and were filming this small ceremony the Admiral was called on to make a speech and so was Wally and I laid the wreath at the memorial stone I was a little embarrassed the wreaths already there were about 3 to 4 feet across and ours was only about 1 foot it looked very small amongst the others. When the laying of the wreaths had been done we held a minutes silence for the victims. I saw a man and a woman at one of the graves the lady was obviously distressed and the man looked grief stricken to. After the ceremony I was ushered over to these people and the interpreter explained to the couple who we were as it transpired they were the parents of one of the victims. The mother was very emotional and could not speak but the father said thank you for bringing there son back and shook my hand. This made all that we had done worthwhile for me and ill never forget the look on the mothers face the grief.

After the visit to the cemetery we were invited to the Navy club to be entertained by the veterans. It was a building close to the naval base where there were rooms for hire and it was obvious that the party we were with was very well respected there. We were led to an area with 2 very large rooms one was set up for a banquet style dinner and was set for a lot of people. As was the norm vodka was brought and the toasts began. During the afternoon we received a phone call from John and Andy who had arrived at the airport.

Our hosts said not to worry and a car was dispatched to pick them up and bring them to the club. While we waited for them we decided to have a pool competition, the table is one I have never seen before the balls only just fitted in the pockets with about 1mm clearance either side consequently the first game went on an on and we gave up I don't think any game was actually finished. When Andy and John arrived this seem to give our hosts an incentive to get them as drunk as we were and more vodka was dispensed. As we approached the time for the meal the room was starting to fill with the invited Russian veterans who were predominantly Navy Divers. It was an honour to be seated at this table with so many heroes of the Soviet Union. These guys had done all the bond spy stuff for real; they looked like the sort of people you wouldn't mess with. It seemed to be the normal procedure to propose a toast, down your vodka, refill your glass, and do it again. There were a lot of toasts during that meal; a good time was had by all. During the drinking I became a knew best friend to one of the Russians and he invited us all downstairs where there was a Sauna this consisted of a changing room, then an entertainment room with a table covered with food and vodka and there was a television and stereo. After this room there was a shower room with two plunge pools one was very cold the other made the first one seem like a warm bath! A door leading of this room led to the sauna. We found out that this was normal type of entertainment for the men lots of testosterone in the air. To my regret I ventured into the sauna which felt like a furnace, at this point our host insisted in beating us with bushes, it is considered a big act of friendship to be beaten to a pulp by your mate in Russia. If this experience has passed you by in your life, I can only describe it as being flailed with red hot coals. I thought I was going to die I lasted about two minutes and had to run for the cold plunge pool (coward that I am) While some of my braver compatriots lasted longer. I did try to get my revenge with the bushes but they loved it, my arms tired quicker than there urge to plunge in the cold pool. Mark had my admiration he decided he would withstand the bushes until Sergie's arms tire, what he did not know was Sergie kept swapping over with Igor. Eventually mark gave in but the state of his back was so bad I thought he might have to go to hospital. I think the amount of drink consumed dulled a lot of the pain. The rest of the evening was spent either in the sauna, plunge pool, entertainment room, or upstairs playing pool or talking with the veterans. It was very late when we returned to our hotel I was just hoping for a lie-in in the morning, Unfortunately that was not to be the case and I duly received my early wake up call to catch the bus for our tour of the city. I managed to drag myself to the shower to invigorate some life back into my abused body. When I eventually came down stairs Phil Sergei and Igor was still standing at the bar, full glass of vodka in hand trying to tempt us to join in. We eventually filled the bus with the correct amount of people and set of with our own personnel tourist guide. First stop was the winter palace we did not have to wait in any queues we just went straight in, I am sorry to say that I am nowhere skilled enough in writing to describe how amazing this building was, if you ever get a chance to visit its well worth it. Outside were a couple in period dress it was the same deal as the church have your photo took for a couple of dollars. Wally and Jimmy were in kilts and this was a talking point for the Russians they all wanted to talk about the kilts, Jimmy even ended up dancing with the lady in period dress in the snow outside it did draw the crowds. We were ushered into the bus, our next stop was the winter palace on the way we stopped at an outside market, we asked if we had time to walk around it was no problem. This market must have sold every conceivable piece of military equipment possible, I had offered to me for $100 a mig fighter helmet, and it was like being in a military quarter master's warehouse. I bought some furry hats for the kids and returned to the bus, after a while we were still missing Paul Mcque. Igor and Sergei were dispatched to find him, and then we saw this Russian Air force Officer crossing the road towards the bus. It turned out to be Paul he had bought himself a whole uniform and put it on, it did look good he didn't get many salutes from the Naval lads though.

The vodka was still flowing and by the time we reached the winter palace there were a few unsteady legs around and Olga (our interpreter) did a good job of holding a couple of them up as we went around the palace. Just like the summer palace this place was breathtaking, the opulence that the rich lived in those days would put to days rich in the shade. When we came out of the palace onto the biggest square I've seen we were accosted again by hawkers this time selling religious Icons we managed to get back to our bus Icon free and we returned to our hotel. The plan was to rest up and we wanted to entertain our hosts. We had organised a room in the hotel, a buffet and the obligatory vodka for the night's festivities. We had talked about this before we had left UK and we brought our duty frees to the party which seemed to be all whiskey. As I mentioned early in the book the Navy and Ruben did not get on to well with each other and we had invited both to the party so we hoped they would burry there differences for the night festivities. Mr Spassky and Admiral Gennady were in attendance these are very important people in Russia so we were well chuffed about that. The party started very sedately as you would expect at this sort of soirée, I was a little concerned that the Ruben restricted themselves to one side of the room and the Russian Navy lads to the other. After a few speeches and vodka toasts we opened the whiskey. Well all I can say is the Russians can drink vodka like water and it appears with little effect on them, whiskey was a different case all together before very long we had some very happy submarine engineers who decided to kick of the singing. We decided that the songs they were singing were to depressing and decided to lighten the atmosphere with a few rugby songs. Though the Russians could not sing along with the songs they did like the beat and before long they were jumping about like Punk Rockers on speed. This was so surreal to watch these normally reserved engineers letting their hair down and really enjoying themselves. The Naval lad eventually came across and we were all enjoying each others company. We played a couple of jokes on the Navy lads, the spoon bashing is where you convince the victim that we had the teaspoon hitting champion with us. Paul Mcque was that person. Paul won't mind me saying he has a slight frame and is not built for fighting. The gauntlet was thrown down to Igor (a powerfully built lad) challenging him to a duel. How it works is a teaspoon is held between the teeth and the opponent bends his head down and you hit him on the head with the teaspoon with your hands are behind your back. Each person takes a turn until one gives up. The rules were explained to Igor and we built up the tension by adding National pride was at stake. To be honest you can not hit very hard with a teaspoon in your mouth it doesn't hurt. We invited Igor to go first he hit Paul on the head, Paul played his part very well and pretended that it was a painful shot and rubbed his head to emphasise the point. When it was Pauls turn to hit Igor when he bent down one of the lads hits Igor on the head with a ladle which is hidden behind his back, this does hurt and Igor thinking he was hit with the teaspoon reacted with great surprise and pain. Normally we all laugh show the victim the ladle and it dawns on him he has been had, even his Russian mates were laughing and thought it a good joke. The trouble was Igor wanted another go and demanded to hit Paul again which he did and we hit him again with the ladle. Igor was now fighting for National pride and wanted to go again. We decided that Igor being the only man in the room not knowing he was being hit on the head with a heavy ladle was so intent on winning the bout that we declared him the winner as Paul could not take the pain anymore. A few more drinking games were played out which mainly consisted of more drinking and getting Russian guests soaking wet, but a good time was had by all. As my senses were being dulled by the whiskey and vodka I do remember sitting with the Admiral and some of his sailors towards the end of the evening and just enjoying there company even though I could not understand the conversation there was a mutual feeling of respect and friendship there. The next morning there was to be a presentation for the Mayo crew Mr Spassky was going to present medals to us. Unfortunately due to the excess of alcohol I was in poor shape and was late. It was only the intervention of a phone call from one of the lads that roused me enough to get dressed and down to the presentation hall in quick time. I arrived just as they called my name out to go up and collect my medal. Once the presentation was completed we were congratulated by our Russian Navy escorts and were made aware of the Navy tradition of blessing the medal, where each of us was given a tumbler of vodka and our medal was then dropped into the glass. The tradition is to then drink the contents of the glass in one go tilting the glass enough to catch the medal in your mouth the medal is then blessed.After the night we had just had this was not a nice experience for us and more than a few had to visit the bathroom afterwards. A few of us were ushered into a large room just of the hall and were interviewed for Russian TV I can't remember to much about it I remember being asked why were we used to recover the Kursk and when I said we were the best inn the world I don't think she was to happy with that. The Russians still believing they recovered the Kursk mostly by themselves. After the presentation and interviews we returned to our rooms to pack for our return flights home. All to fast our visit was coming to an end and it was time to leave. We congregated in the foyer of the hotel to say our goodbyes, we hugged and promised to keep in touch and all too soon we were on the bus heading for the airport Andrei came with us on the bus and we were whisked through customs and before we knew it we were flying back to U.K. The flight was a chance to catch up on some much needed sleep and we all took full advantage.

POST SCRIPT

Since returning to work my days working on the Mayo was numbered I was due to transfer with most of my colleagues to another vessel Seven Pelican. The Mayo was deemed surplus to requirements in the North Sea and was dispatched to Brazil for work in the region. Later she was dispatched to Angola where I was asked to join her for a quick job repairing a water injection line. This went well and the Mayo performed up to her usual high standard. , it was nice to be back onboard. Rumour was rife that the company had decided to sell her which is a shame she is a good vessel. Later these rumours were realised and she was sold to an Egyptian company PMS (Petroleum Marine Services) She sailed away it was sad to see her go.

Late 2004 I was asked if I would join the Mayo in Egypt for a one of job, there had been a blow out on the Temsha platform and the Mayo was tasked to re-route existing pipelines around the platform. I joined the Mayo on the 10th of January 2005 it was only going to be a 1 month trip it would be the last time I would ever see her again. Unfortunately she had been left to deteriorate no money was spent on her and she was dying fast. I completed my month on her and returned to UK what a sad end to my relationship with her. I wish her all the best for the future.

ACKNOWLEDGMENTS

I would like to thank the people who helped me with this book, there drive and patience was an inspiration.

W Smickersgill. For his research, and writing assistance.

Sue Hale. Who tirelessly transcribed my ramblings from my Dictaphone.

Wally Wallace & Mark Girdlestone. for their contributions.

The guys on the vessel who kept asking "when is the book coming out"

And finally the Mayo crew who helped provide the material

A Final Acknowledgement for the Norwegian Cutting company, the Dutch yard who worked tirelessly to convert the barge, Mammoet workforce who was on the lift barge and finally the Russian Navy and Engineers without any of these people I am sure the outcome would not have been as successful.